IT'S OK TO BE GAY

STRAIGHT TALK ABOUT HOMOSEXUALITY FOR GAY PEOPLE AND THOSE WHO LOVE THEM

SEAN LEMSON

S LEMSON PUBLISHING

S Lemson Publishing

First edition January 2020

To inquire about guest speaking engagements, please contact
speakers@seanlemson.com.

Manufactured in the United States of America

Cover Design: J. Cole
Photography: Carlo Delumpa

ISBN 978-1-7330042-0-6
ISBN 978-1-7330042-1-3 (e-book)
ISBN 978-1-733042-2-0 (audio book)

DEDICATION

This book is dedicated to "Daryl". In Chapter 7: Homosexuality and Religion, you will read about a boy I called Daryl. Daryl's story perfectly captures the experience of too many LGBT youth on this planet. The goal for the rest of my life is to make sure that stories like Daryl's never happen again.

To my mom, who was always a trailblazer of acceptance and courage. Cancer took her body. Dementia took her mind. Nothing could take her love for me, or mine for her.

Lastly, to my husband, team mate, and partner Jesse. You and I have been there for each other for over 15 years. You're an inspiration to me. Having you by my side and being by yours continues to be the biggest honor of my life.

ACKNOWLEDGEMENTS

I have been working on this book with varying levels of dedication for almost a decade. Life has a way of creating obstacles for our goals sometimes and I was taken off track several times. Each time I picked it back up and began again, I was always surprised by how timeless the information in it seemed to be. Coming to terms with homosexuality in all its forms hasn't changed much in the past ten years, but it is my hope that one day, long after I'm gone, someone picks this book up in a yard sale and says, "Wow, books like this were needed back then?"

To make sure I got it published before that day, I owe a great deal of gratitude to Marcia Norris. Her gentle prodding over the years and her coaching through the business of self-publishing and promotion was invaluable.

Once I thought it was perfect, I sent the manuscript to Brook Warner who connected me with a development coach and a copyeditor. Each showed me how much better it could be and

I'm forever thankful for their excellent feedback. Any remaining errors belong to me.

I'd also like to acknowledge the importance of my promise to Neale Donald Walsch. His admonishment and guidance, which you will read about in the book, were important beacons that never let me get away with leaving the finish line uncrossed.

Finally, I'd like to thank all of my bullies. You made my life miserable in High School, but you also created a platform for me to build my self-esteem on top of. Although I got away from all of you, my hope is that you found peace with who you were back then and have learned to be better people as adults today. I forgive you.

ABOUT THE COVER

Getting the cover designed for this book was an inspirational and humbling exercise. I created a contest on a graphic design website and I got nearly 100 submissions! They came with notes that said things like, "I did this one personally, not professionally. I needed a book like this when I was growing up." These kinds of comments warmed my heart and reminded me why I wrote the book in the first place.

The winning entry, designed by J. Cole, was chosen because that kid on the front was me growing up. Trying to paint his own reality until finally painting onto life's canvas that it's OK to be gay. He's standing defiant. Strong. Messy but determined. My heart skipped a beat when I saw that image. It's my hope that this book inspires you to pick up that paint brush and get to work on your own life's canvas. Start by painting the words "It's OK to Be Gay."

Contents

IT'S OK TO BE GAY

Introduction

It's OK to be gay. This would be a short book if I could type those five words and have you believe it, but you picked up this book because perhaps you don't believe that statement. Perhaps homosexuality is causing you some grief—either because you are gay or because someone you care about is gay and you're not OK with it. Helping you accept your own or someone else's homosexuality is a goal for me with this book, but I do have higher aspirations for what we'll accomplish together. This is also about being OK with being you. As you'll soon see, that applies to you whether you are the gay person or a person in his or her life.

We shouldn't dive too far into this whole "It's OK to be gay" thing until we get something out of the way. Let's put aside gay or straight for right now and focus on just this raw question:

Do you feel that everyone has a right to be happy?

It might surprise you how many people don't feel like they have a right to be happy. It's like they're stuck in a dark room, and instead of looking for a light switch, they just give up and resign themselves to darkness. If this is you, then we're going to have an uphill battle in the coming chapters because everything I say will get a "Yeah, but" response from you. In order for me to have a chance to successfully convince you that it's OK for you or a loved one to be gay, you first have to accept and acknowledge that we're all entitled to feeling OK in general. If you're unhappy and some portion of that unhappiness stems from you or someone you love being gay, this book can help. All I ask is that you open your mind to the possibility that, one way or another, we are all entitled to being happy with who we really are. It's OK if you're skeptical, but if you have a closed mind about that, you will struggle with this material.

I do have one logistical writing issue to discuss, and that is my use of the word "gay." For simplicity, I will use the words "gay" and "homosexual" interchangeably. I will not get into assigning genders to the word "gay" unless I'm making a point that involves just one gender. So, when you read "gay," you can assume it applies to gay men and lesbian women as well as the same-gender attraction portion of bisexuality.

Gay Readers

Whether you're still closeted, freshly free from it, or have been out for many years, you may still be struggling with an inner conflict about your homosexuality. Sometimes it's the people in your life who have this problem. This book is for both audiences because there's something about acceptance that's both personal and universal. Whether your tension is in your home life, your family, your job, your social life, or your church, you may believe that one or all of these areas of life are conspiring against your acceptance of being gay. This book will help. While there are a few chapters specifically intended for one audience or the other, I believe everyone will get something from reading the whole thing.

Now would be a good time for a standard disclaimer, however. I'm not promising that after you read this, your family is going to love the fact that you're gay, that your church will accept you, that people will stop teasing you at school, or that you'll get the respect you deserve at work. That would be a tall order for any book. Instead, my goal is to help you understand the paths those around you are choosing—even if those paths mean not accepting you. I also hope to empower you with a change of perspective that might make any struggles you're currently facing seem less menacing. Doing all this requires you to disconnect your opinion of yourself from the opinion others have about you, and we'll take that journey together in these pages.

Straight Readers

Although I sometimes appear to be speaking directly to gay men and women, there is much to be learned by straight readers either who have just recently learned that someone they care about is gay or who just wish to learn more about the topic. The Dog

Whisperer, Cesar Millan, says that we often get the dog we need instead of the dog we want. When viewed metaphorically, I believe that life is this way also. If you've recently learned that someone you care about is gay, you've been presented with a wonderful opportunity to decide who you are in relation to that. If you're uncomfortable, learning what's behind your discomfort may teach you more about yourself than the topic of homosexuality.

You may have the belief that if you object strongly enough—if you really make it clear how much you disapprove of your loved one's homosexuality—they will "wake up" and become straight. Some parents up the ante all the way to kicking their gay son or daughter out onto the street with the hope that they'll get the point that homosexuality will not be "tolerated in this household". We'll get into this in more detail later, but that would be the equivalent of telling your blond child, "We do not tolerate blond people in this household." He may dye his hair black to make you happy (read: comfortable) and to keep a roof over his head, but he'll still be a kid with blond roots, and now he's got the added stress of hiding them from you. My goal for this audience is that you learn enough about homosexuality to challenge some of the perceptions and ideas you may have about it now. The fact that you're holding this book is already demonstrating a willingness to consider a different perspective, and I applaud you for that.

The Structure of the Book

The book is made up of four parts:
- Part One: Tools to Open a Mind
- Part Two: Homosexuality Basics
- Part Three: Accepting Others
- Part Four: Accepting Yourself

To be honest, I really struggled with whether to include Part One in the book at all. Entire books have been written about being open-minded and accepting—including the Bible, a book that is often used against gays. My decision to include it came from my belief that some of us have forgotten how to really open our minds. If I don't pay some attention to how we form our realities, prejudices, and perspectives, I'll be doing a disservice to the rest of the book. That material is going to challenge you to see things in a new way, and if you don't understand how you formed your old way, you won't believe that it's possible to change it.

Here's the conundrum: we all do what makes sense to us. That means you probably think you *are* open-minded and correct about most everything in your life. Because of that, you may be tempted to skip Part One. I advise you not to. It will help for you to understand how your mind works. It's an auto-piloting, efficient thought rocket that can draw conclusions at a blistering speed. As you'll see, that's not going to be to your benefit when challenging old beliefs about the world.

Part Two gets some of the basics about homosexuality out of the way. We'll dive right in and dispel some of the myths surrounding gays and homosexuality in general. After that, we'll make an attempt at defining what it means to be gay from a biological and evolutionary standpoint and discuss sexuality as a spectrum. As part of the basics, we must discuss the ways homosexuality is treated in the media, including TV and Hollywood. We'll cover the struggle for gay rights and then finish the section with a socially forbidden discussion about religion.

Part Three is about accepting others. In that section, we'll cover what it's like being gay during the various stages of social development. Then we'll talk about being the parent of a gay son or daughter. We'll round out the chapter with a discussion of what to do if you suspect your son or daughter is being bullied.

Part Four is to help gay readers become comfortable in their own skin. We'll discuss internalized homophobia (yes, that's a thing) and the process of coming out. We'll finish the book with a discussion about fighting for a life worth living.

So, Who the Heck Am I?

As a gay male born in the early '70s, I grew up on the west coast of the United States and was spared some of the horrors that so many of my gay brothers and sisters suffered before me. My generation didn't have to tolerate public television campaigns against homosexuality and the scientific ignorance that drove the unethical and morally questionable "treatments" in the 1950s. We didn't suffer the widespread, open police brutality of the late 1960s.

Instead, we were the generation of "Don't ask, don't tell." As young adults, we were basically told, "Fine, be gay. Just keep it to yourself." While we were being asked to remain closeted, the commercial Internet was born, which opened up channels of communication from one closet to another, but it also brought the hatred right to our computer screens.

As the Internet began to slowly whittle away at whatever notion we all had about privacy, being closeted became frighteningly difficult to maintain. Social media created even more land mines for closeted gays. It also made bullying of gay teens even more pervasive and invasive.

As someone who's grown up in this time and place, I've got a good view of where we came from and where we're going. I'm not a young man of the 1950s, '60s, or even '70s, so I'm not a war-torn veteran in the battle for gay rights. Instead, I'm hoping my generation is the bridge between those tumultuous times and a time that allows gay people to step out of our closets and be loved for who we are.

There's a great deal of misconception and misinformation about homosexuality out there. It's spread in subtle and not-so-subtle ways. My job here is to connect you to real information. If, along the way, that shifts your position—even a little bit—I'll be happy. If it prevents one gay teen suicide or one homeless gay kid, my mission will be fulfilled.

It's my hope that by honestly and openly sharing my experience growing up over the next few pages, you'll take the first steps towards understanding those around you regardless of whether the closet door has your name on it or someone's you love. These experiences are the impetus for me writing this book. I'm thrilled beyond words that you're reading it right now.

Born Gay

My earliest sexual memories go back to the age of five. I remember that, even at that early age, I was fantasizing about the boys in my neighborhood. I was still many years from any hormonal assistance in this matter, but I remember the attraction like it was yesterday. I was also acting on this, even going so far as to get caught red-handed in the shed with some of the neighbor kids, all of us with our pants down.

Looking back on all this, I can say with certainty that my five-year-old brain didn't see this as sexual at all. It just felt good and made things . . . uh . . . happen for me physically that I couldn't really describe. For every bit of my childhood, I had these types of experiences. I'm not a doctor, but sleepovers usually resulted in me playing one when I was a kid. Clearly, these homosexual attractions were strong, natural, and with me long before I consciously began thinking about them as sexual at all.

Throughout my childhood and adolescence, I had lots of male celebrity crushes. One that I can remember vividly was Shaun Cassidy. (Go google it, kids. I'll wait.) I was obsessed with him from age seven. I'm sure my parents thought it was because I shared his name, but that was not it at all. I also had crushes on Kirk Cameron (who ironically has grown into quite a homophobic adult), Wil Wheaton, and Jonathan Brandis (who tragically committed suicide in 2003). These crushes were not really sexual attractions. I don't recall thinking much about these stars in a sexual way at all. When I say crushes, I mean something different. Something giddy. As close as a seven-to-ten-year-old could get to romantic love. I fantasized about romantic dates, not sex. Notably absent during all these years was any of those feelings for girls or women. I never made a choice about this. It just . . . was, and always has been. More on that in a bit.

Adolescence

Once my hormones kicked into full gear, my sexual behavior and that of my friends did also. But my friends were going after girls, and I was going after my friends. My life during this time was very emotionally difficult. I was closeted, having sexual experiences with my friends (who were probably just happy to get the relief from their constant, sometimes involuntary erections), and falling deeply in love with some of them. I fell for one after another just as they were falling for girls.

The jealousy raged in me when they would go on dates or go to school dances while I sat home pretending not to care, completely disinterested in girls. To say that I repeatedly had my heart broken in junior high and high school would be an understatement. I had no healthy, publicly acceptable outlet for my emotional attractions. So instead I usually wept or fumed in private. Sometimes, I would act as the go-between for my crushes and the girls they were interested in. It was as if I was living vicariously through those girls' experiences with these boys I wanted for myself. It was a painful time for me because jealousy was constantly present.

One night when I was a sophomore, a boy I had a crush on spent the night at my house. We were lying next to each other, and I gently laid my hand on his side. It was a motion I could have easily retracted and explained away if he said anything . . . but he didn't. Things escalated, and we both had a good experience, at least I thought so. The next morning, he went to school and started telling everyone that I was gay and that he had rebuffed me when I made a move on him the night before. That single event changed my life.

Brené Brown often describes the difference between guilt and shame this way: guilt is "I *made* a mistake," and shame is "I *am* a mistake." This was the first time I felt like I *was* a mistake. I had kids walking past me between classes asking me, "Do you get hard-ons in the locker room?" The teasing was relentless, and people began avoiding me. It was clear that whatever was driving this behavior, it needed to be kept secret, and I'd need to be much more cautious moving forward.

Later that year, I met a boy, a bit of a loner like me. We hit it off and quickly became best friends. Over time, we experimented sexually, and I came to have real feelings for him that I always described as "best friend" feelings. One day in our senior year, we were working on his truck stereo and he asked if I wanted to spend the night. I said yes, and he cheered, "Yay! My boyfriend is going to stay over!" We laughed, and the usual sexual activities happened that night, but there was something different, something more emotional happening as well. I think this may have been the first time I made love to someone. I never got to find out where this was leading. Several weeks later, he was killed in a car accident.

I was devastated. I mourned the loss of my best friend, but many years later, I admitted that I was really mourning the loss of my first boyfriend. I'll never know if he was really gay or just experimenting with his sexuality during a time when many do just that. I have regrets for being in the closet, but my biggest is never being able to tell him how much I loved him while he was alive. Those words just couldn't penetrate the closet door.

When I read that gay teens commit suicide at much higher rates than straight teens, I know exactly why. It's this feeling of being alone, unable to be honest with those you love, unable to talk to anyone about the jealousy and shame you feel. It's also a time when you feel like you'll never meet anyone to love, while everyone around you is seemingly having no difficulties with that. Add to that an unprecedented ability for kids to bully each other online and, in some parts of the country, an increased religious fervor determined to purge homosexuality from society, and you have a recipe for the kinds of elevated suicide rates we're seeing in the LGBT teen community. If this describes you right now, stay with me. I have some hopeful news.

Young Adulthood

After I turned eighteen, I immediately moved out of my mom's house to go to school in Los Angeles. I still believed I was straight and was just slow to grow out of this "phase." I continued to have crushes on a few classmates, but my sexual activity slowed way down. Since I was an adult then, living on my own, I decided to get a rental account at a video store down the street from my house. (For my younger readers, a video store was a place we went to rent VHS tapes for our VCRs. What's a VCR? Oh, never mind.) They had an adult section, and I wandered in to take a look. It was the first time I'd ever seen anything like it. I immediately gravitated to the gay section, which I hadn't even known existed. The guys were so much more attractive to me.

I grabbed a couple of gay videos that looked good and very trepidatiously approached the front counter, where a kid my age was working. He saw the titles and started laughing. He walked away to get the movies while shaking his head. I remember feeling so much shame welling up in me. It's like someone ripped off the fresh scab from high school and poured salt right on the wound. There I was, legally an adult, feeling like a child who'd just been pantsed in front of his classmates.

This experience made me even less willing to be associated with "gay" anything. It didn't make me any less attracted to guys; it just made me less likely to call that "gay" and less likely to be open about it. It created a cognitive dissonance in my life that lasted for years.

Adulthood

In my early twenties, I continued to fall madly in love with straight guys. It created this weird dynamic in my social circles. Many of my friendships were actually slow, persistent pickups in progress. My mom would later comment, after I came out, that she thought it was strange that all my friends were so good-looking. When she said this, I experienced what I can only call sheepish pride. *At least I have good taste,* I thought to myself.

One such particularly good-looking friend was a guy I met at work. We hit it off, and I'd venture to say that he would have described himself as "bi-curious." Bi-curious basically means straight with a curiosity about having sex with the same gender. However, let's call it one half step away from bisexuality because bisexuality has an emotional component to it that bi-curious people do not claim to have. For them, it's mostly described as a physical attraction. Instead of discussing it openly, we did all kinds of sexual things at night when we could both pretend to be asleep and not talk about it in the morning. I know it might sound weird, but the mind works in mysterious ways and plausible (or sometimes implausible) deniability is common in these situations.

While we were both enjoying ourselves physically, I was falling head over heels in love with him. One Christmas, I decided to buy him a necklace. My mom helped me pick it out. Looking back on this, I can see how obviously gay I was, but I continued to insist that we were just that good of friends. After I gave him the necklace, he freaked out. I think it was the moment it became clear to both of us that our feelings were lopsided. Shortly thereafter, he moved across the country, and I never saw or heard from him again. Imagine the lessons I was learning about falling in and expressing love, and the difference between love and physical attraction. Each time I took an emotional risk, I was rejected or suffered a loss. This greatly set me back in my journey towards coming out.

Coming Out

A few years later, I found myself living in Las Vegas with my best friend at the time, a recently divorced woman who was the first person I ever confessed to being bisexual to. In my case, this would later be known as the "bi now, gay later" program. It was a way for me to put one foot out of the closet and keep the other inside. Bisexuality *is* a real thing, however, as we'll discuss in more detail in Chapter 4: What Does It Mean to Be Gay?

As I mentioned earlier, I belong to the generation of "Don't Ask, Don't Tell," and during this time, President Clinton was advocating this very plan to the US military, so it was the topic of the news almost every day. I was sitting in a work van with a coworker eating lunch, and the topic came up in conversation. He began railing against gay people. "These faggots need to either choose to be straight or get out of the military." I protested as much as a closeted gay person could. I told him that perhaps it wasn't a choice for them, and didn't they still have the right to serve their country if they wanted to?

"Bullshit. They're queer. They deserve what they're getting for choosing something so unnatural."

When I got home from work that night, I cried. But for the first time, I wasn't crying because I was gay, I was crying because I couldn't say anything to defend myself or other gays because I was in the closet. I was so frustrated by my inability to say, "You know what? I'm gay. I'll bet you didn't know that because your version of gay is defined by a narrow stereotype. And because I'm gay I can tell you definitively I didn't *choose* to be gay. You don't know anything about me or my childhood, but if you did, you'd know that *no one* would choose to go through what I did."

After the tears dried and I talked it out with my friend, I made the decision to come out. I had a trip back home scheduled, and I decided to start with my mom. When I got there, I sat down with her and told her I was gay. To my surprise, she said, "Sean, I was waiting for you to tell me." She gave me a long hug, and we both cried.

It felt like someone had just lifted a ton of bricks off of my shoulders. People say that all the time, but this was the first time I'd experienced it. I felt lighter. Empowered. Comfortable in my own skin for the first time.

A fairly common experience for many gay males is a hesitation to tell the older males in their family. I was no exception. My older brother and my dad were the last to be told, and I never told my grandfather, even though I'm fairly certain he figured it out before he died when he kept seeing the same "friend" show up at family events.

My grandmother, even though she did know, still referred to my partner of nearly eight years at the time as my "friend." She has since passed away, and I know she loved my partner and me, but I always felt a little pang of pain when she referred to him as "my friend." I wonder if we had been permitted to have a real wedding before she died, would she have been more likely to call him my husband?

Onward

There are many, many stories to tell about my life from that point until now. I'll interject some of them as we go through the material to drive home major points, but this isn't an autobiography. The main thing I've learned from being closeted and ashamed of who I was for so many years is that my life's purpose is to help people live authentically and deliberately. I have set the lofty goal that the rest of this book will help you do this whether you're straight, gay, or something in between.

Part One:
Tools to Open a Mind

"When we are no longer able to change a situation, we are challenged to change ourselves."

– Viktor Frankl

Chapter 1: Your Mind. Friend or Foe?

"We don't see things as they are, we see them as we are."

— Anaïs Nin

Whether you are gay or straight, you're likely reading this book because you're not OK with your own homosexuality or someone else's. Perhaps you believe that homosexuality is a sin or unnatural. That is your reality about it. Yet at some level, you must be doubtful about that conclusion. Not everyone sees homosexuality in this way. What do they know that you don't? Could they be right? In this chapter, I aim to show you that it isn't so much *what* a person's conclusion about homosexuality is, but more *how* they came to it. Much of it is automatic, as we'll see, but that doesn't mean it's unchangeable.

Movie Magic

My stepfather is a retired crane operator. When I was a young man, I joined him at the site of one of his jobs—the filming of a movie in San Francisco. There was a bus on its side with stuntmen inside strapped to cables that were attached to his crane. When the director yelled, "Action!" my stepdad was to lift these people out of the bus through the broken windows as if they were spirits being released from their bodies. I asked him, "What do they do about the cables in the finished film?" He said they'd erase them digitally afterwards. When I watched the movie, I remember recalling that day with my stepdad and remembering what he told me. The whole scene took on new meaning to me because I knew how it was done.

The lesson I learned from that experience is that once someone explains the "trick" behind something, it's difficult to be willfully fooled by it again. My hope is that if I show you *how* your brain reaches conclusions, it will become difficult for you to end up with a conclusion you do not intend or wish to have. The "magic" behind it will have been revealed. The only way you could be fooled moving forward is if you allowed yourself to be.

What I'm about to share with you is the process by which you go from an event or piece of information to a reality for yourself. An entire book could be written about this topic and, in fact, has been. Many of the concepts that follow are from the book by Neale Donald Walsch entitled, *When Everything*

Changes, Change Everything.[1] If this information interests you, I strongly encourage you to read that book to see how these same concepts can be used to help you change your reality on any issue. I had the honor of meeting Neale and learning these concepts from him directly. The book you're holding is a direct result of a commitment I made to him to write it. I'm overjoyed to be able to share this information with you because I really do view it as the secret to happiness. How's that for a setup?

Reality Magic

Many people believe that life happens *to* them and their reality is simply an outcome of the events that occur in their lives. This simple model looks like Figure 1 below:

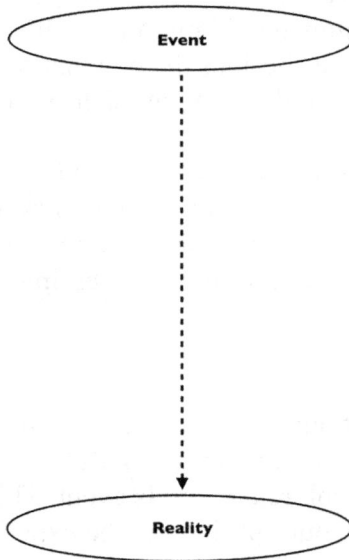

Figure 1

---

[1] Neale Donald Walsch, *When Everything Changes, Change Everything* (Ashland: EmNin, 2009).

In fact, that direct line doesn't exist. If it did, we'd all end up at the same reality from the same event.

It may surprise you to consider that there is more than one reality to be had in the first place. Reality is a highly subjective concept. For example, consider the headline, "Republicans Win the White House!" Is that good news or bad news? Well, in fact, it's neither. It's just news. Whether it's good news or bad news depends on your own personal political views. Four different people could experience four completely different realities about that same event. As another example, rain in the forecast could be terrible news if you were planning a camping trip but great news if you're a farmer.

I don't personally find this multiple-reality thing scary; I find it liberating because it means I have a choice in many of the situations where it's tempting to feel like I don't. This isn't a "whistling past the graveyard" mind trick. It's a genuine effort to be open to perspectives besides the one that's leading to me feeling sad, angry, scared, or any number of other negative emotions.

Changing our realities is about understanding the mechanics behind what made them in the first place. Make no mistake, there *is* a process that all human beings go through to create our realities. The first stop is accessing our memory (data) about similar events.

Data

Data is simply what our past has given our minds to work with about this event. It's our memories of all the events we've had or witnessed that we think relate to this event. This data comes from personal experience, our upbringing, the experiences of others we've observed, the media, and other outside and inside influences. Our memories about gay people are loaded with influence from outside sources. The media, our parents, our religions, our communities, and perhaps a past encounter with a gay person or someone we thought was gay all contribute to our overall data about homosexuality. Some of this data feeds our opinions, and many of us are walking around with a very distorted set of concepts about homosexuality (and life) as a result. In order to change that, we must challenge that data (thoughts and memories) for accuracy and truth. Making a reality from bad data is like making a recipe using bad ingredients. It won't resemble the picture in the cookbook.

Truth

From this data, our mind forms our *truth* about that event. Think of truth as the seed from which our opinion of the event grows, before we've had a chance to think about it. It is a shortcut for our brains. When something resembling this event happened to us the first time, we practically had to become Sherlock Holmes to "figure out" how to react and what reality to have around that event. We do this a lot as children when many events are new experiences. The result of all this work is a "truth" about that event. To conserve energy and save time, our minds will pattern match new events into similar events from our past (stored data) so that we can use one of our previous "truths" to avoid all that detective work.

Thought

From our truth, we form a *thought*. This stage is the first time we would hear a voice in our heads "saying" something to us. It's the same voice we hear all day. The one that says, "There's never a cop around when you need one," and all the rest of our thoughts. Just realize that before that voice came around, we've already done two things: accessed our data and pattern matched a truth about that data. Thought is like the narrative that neatly sums up the truth we matched. For example, "There it is again, someone blaming me. It's always *my* fault. Why can't people accept their own responsibility when they're clearly wrong?" It's at this point in the process that we will form our *perspective* about the event. More about that shortly.

Emotion

The thought we create has *emotions* attached to it. The "color" of these emotions (whether it be positive, negative, or indifferent) is baggage we attached back at the data stage because the memories have that color stored with them. We might experience anger or fear (fight or flight). We might also experience frustration, judgment, sadness, or a plethora of different emotions. What's important to notice is that the data, truth, and thought that led us here are being magnified by the emotions we attach at this stage. This is when a thought we're annoyed to be having might turn into hate or rage.

Experience

Depending on whether we've attached positive, negative, or indifferent emotions determines how we *experience* the event. It will influence whether we describe the event as positive or negative or something else. It could reinforce our victim story, cause laughter, trigger lashing out, or a variety of other experiences. The experience will almost certainly mirror, or be a reaction to, the one we had when the original experience occurred that created the data, truth, thought, and emotion in our past.

Reality

Our experience becomes our *reality* about the event. Think of our reality as the "place" we are after the experience (the collection of emotions, how our mood is affected, etc.).

Let's start by redrawing that diagram now with our new information (see Figure 2):

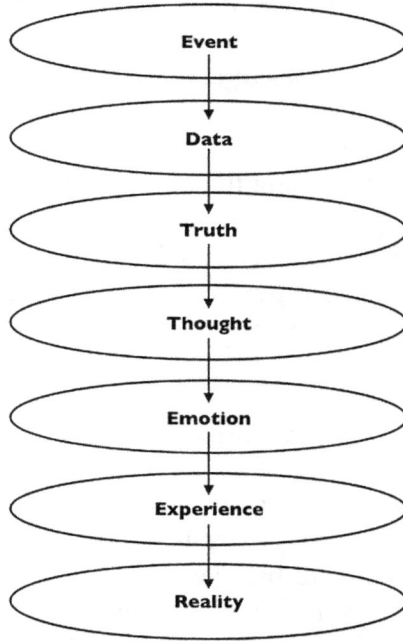

Figure 2

Data Comes in Two Flavors

Even Figure 2 is a bit oversimplified, so stay with me here while I add a few additional details. Recall that the data portion of this process is our mind trying to pattern match the event with previous events using our memory. The data our minds work with comes in two flavors: factual and judged.

Factual data is analogous to the images a video camera would have recorded. The camera has no judgment about what it records; it just records "what is so." If I observe my father slap my mother as a child, factual data would be simply that my father slapped my mother.

Judged data is what happens when we attach any feeling, thought, or judgment (based on past experience, upbringing, the media, etc.) to that factual data.

In the example above, if I observe my father slap my mother as a child, and I viewed my mom as a victim, or if I viewed my father as vicious or abusive, I'd be working with judged data. Judged data isn't bad in and of itself. As we'll soon see, however, it removes a lot of the choice we have about what kind of reality we have about the event. Now would be a good time for me to tell you that choosing factual data does *not* inherently remove your ability to see an event as "wrong" or "bad." It just allows more flexibility to choose how you think, feel, and experience the event.

Truth Comes in Three Flavors

Truths also come in several varieties: actual, apparent, or imaginary.

Actual truth is what is true from the universe's perspective. Call it the deeper truth—perhaps one you do not consciously even know or believe. It's as if you could see the event from the perspective of a nonjudgmental viewpoint. Perhaps you see the beauty in the event from this elevation no matter how heinous it is. It's way beyond the scope of this book for me to delve deeply into what actual truth means, but Walsch does a nice job of it, so check out his book for more detail. One simple way to think of this is to imagine a white crayon on the table. If you were to look at that crayon through yellow lenses, you'd see a yellow crayon, but the *actual truth* is that the crayon is white. Objectively it's white, subjectively it's yellow. If we turned off the lights completely, you may not see the crayon at all. But the *actual truth* is that there is still a white crayon there, and it is that color whether you see it or not. There is a UPS driver coming up the street. The fact that your dog can hear it and you can't doesn't mean it isn't true. That's actual truth.

Apparent truth is like an unbiased observer of that video recording telling you what they're seeing, free of any judgment. Like a court reporter reading from the transcript of a court proceeding, this truth has no vested interest in the outcome and is merely describing—without judgment—the event in question. Unlike actual truth, apparent truth requires the senses. Because of that there is some level of subjectivity involved even if it's minor. Our court reporter still has inflections in her voice at certain words even though she's trying to be objective. Freedom from judgment doesn't mean freedom from subjectivity. She may be unwittingly looking through those yellow lenses so she will report the crayon as yellow but there will be no attempt to attach judgment to the color.

Imaginary truth is as though a biased observer (someone with prejudices, preconceptions, or stereotypes) is detailing that same video recording. Imaginary truth is like the devil or angel sitting on your shoulder describing the event in question. It also contains a bunch of imagined motives such as "She's just doing this because she's jealous," or "He obviously doesn't love his kids."

Reality Comes in Three Flavors

Lastly, there are three types of reality: ultimate, observed, and distorted.

Ultimate reality is the reality from the universe's perspective. That nonjudgmental, lens-free observer has a reality about the event, and that reality is the ultimate reality. ("There is a white crayon on the table even though you can't see it.")

Observed reality is the reality we arrive at if we listen to that court reporter. We will see the event as an event, nothing more, nothing less. ("The crayon is yellow." Then, if someone turns the light off, "The room is dark.")

Distorted reality is where we arrive when we take the path of the biased observer. ("There was a yellow crayon on the table but someone turned off the lights because they don't want you to see it.")

The most important thing to take away at this point is that we aren't stuck with the reality we have, and there's a very strong possibility that the one we've got is distorted. To understand why that is, we need to understand how these pathways work.

Pathways to Reality

Factual data has a pathway that can lead to actual truth or to apparent truth, but judged data always leads to imaginary truth. Once we're on one of those three paths down the chain through thought, emotion, and experience, our reality is assured. It's like taking an exit off the highway. Whether we intended to or not, we're committed.

Each of the three truth types determines how we will experience the reality of the event. Actual truth leads to ultimate reality, apparent truth leads to observed reality, and imaginary truth leads to distorted reality. Take a look at Figure 3 below to see these pathways:

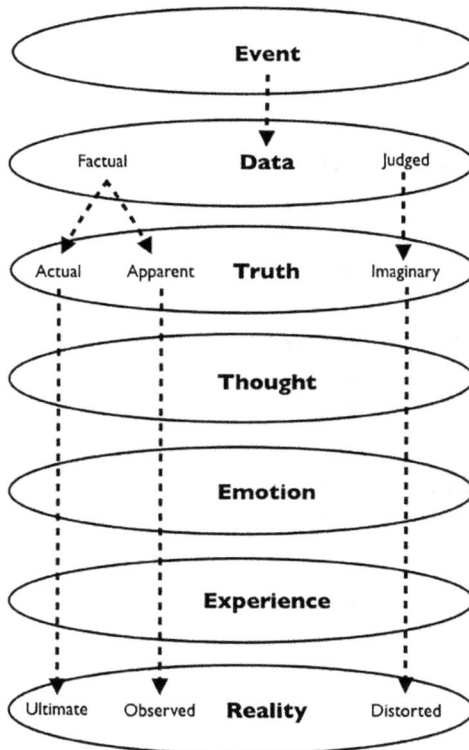

Figure 3

Example: Three Paths to Reality

Now that we've determined that our reality about an event is actually the product of a series of stops our brains make, I want to explore what the various paths might look like for three fictional people who all witness the same event and have three completely different realities about it. I admit that the example is a bit contrived, but it will serve our purpose for the moment.

The Observers

Mary, fifty, was raised in a religious home, but her parents were careful to let her explore and interpret the world in the way that made sense to her. Because of this, Mary took an interest in Buddhism in college and found its teachings to be liberating. Over many years of practice, she has taught herself to keep her perspective as high as possible. As a result, she always strives to see the lessons and opportunities in all the events that happen in her life.

Jake is a straight twenty-four-year-old college student. He has several good friends who are gay, and homosexuality has never bothered him. When he was in high school, he even sexually experimented with a few of his friends but figured out that it wasn't who he was. He eventually plans to marry his girlfriend of three years.

Fred is thirty-five. Like Mary, Fred grew up in a religious household but he was taught that homosexuality is the devil working his ways on humanity. Fred was molested as a child by a man in his family that he looked up to. Being forced to keep quiet about that has caused him a great deal of pain and fear that he stuffs away. For Fred, that pain and fear manifests as a hatred for gay people. As a way to justify his hatred to himself and others, he focuses deeply on the parts of the Bible that he believes condemn homosexuality as unnatural and sinful. Fred's dad always pressured him to have a stiff upper lip and refrain from crying when hurt. Whenever Fred saw an effeminate gay man on TV, it reinforced his belief that all gay men lack masculinity and are weak.

The Event

Fred, Jake, and Mary do not know each other and are each walking separately down the same street, which opens into a park. On a park bench in the distance, they all see two men holding hands and laughing. One gives the other a peck on the cheek, which leads to a longer and more affectionate kiss, followed by more giggling. In microseconds, the three observers search their memories for how to make sense of the event.

The Data Decision

Neither Mary nor Jake have much judged data about homosexuality, so they connect what they see on the park bench that day to factual data: two men are holding hands and kissed each other.

Fred, on the other hand, has a whole bunch of judged data about homosexuality. Some might argue he's almost obsessed with it. As a result, Fred will seemingly unwillingly choose the judged data pathway.

Fred, Jake, and Mary's decision to choose factual or judged data is a major part of the process. For better or worse, the path they choose sets the stage for the rest of the chain reaction all the way down. Referring to Figure 3 on page 24, you can see that it's impossible for Fred to have anything but a distorted reality once he goes down the judged data path.

This is the nature of things, and it makes perfect sense. Choosing judged data is like looking at the white crayon through the yellow lenses. The crayon is white (factual), but you're seeing yellow (judged). No matter what happens all the way down the line, your reality will be distorted by yellow in some capacity.

When Fred chooses judged data about the two men on the park bench and the judgment attached to that data is harsh, hateful, fearful, or spiteful, his reality will ultimately be distorted by those emotions. By matching factual data, Jake and Mary have a lot more control over what their reality looks like. The three of them are going to take three separate paths to form three separate realities, and we're going to continue to follow each starting with Mary.

Mary's Path (Factual Data, Actual Truth, Ultimate Reality)

Mary tends to see things from a higher perspective. Her data is the same as Jake's: these two men are kissing and holding hands with one another. But Mary sees the actual truth in the situation. She sees that we're all "in this together" and that love is love regardless of which genders it appears between. She feels a "connectedness" with everything around her and shares in the love these two are feeling for each other. She walks on feeling warmth and happiness (her reality).

Jake's Path (Factual Data, Apparent Truth, Observed Reality)

For Jake, seeing these two men be affectionate on the park bench is no different than a man and a woman doing so. Jake's truth about the event is very observational: these two men are kissing and holding hands with one another. This is Jake's apparent truth. It's apparent because it's still being viewed through the perspective of Jake with all the limitations that come from that (for example, his distance from the bench could obscure some part of the event for him).

      Jake's first thought about the event (which happens milliseconds after seeing it) is that these two men seem to really love each other, or at minimum, enjoy each other's company. Jake and his girlfriend share experiences just like this from time to time, and he begins to feel a longing to be with her. His experience about the whole event ends up being an appreciation for how much he loves his girlfriend. Jake ends up at an observed reality, which is simply that two people who love each other are showing affection. He uses this reality to text his girlfriend to tell her he loves her.

Fred's Path (Judged Data, Imaginary Truth, Distorted Reality)

Fred's path begins with the large laundry list of judged data discussed above. From that, he lands on an imaginary truth. It is imaginary not because his data is "right" or "wrong." It's imaginary because it projects imagery from *his* past *onto* these two men seated on the park bench.

Neither of these men are the man who molested him. They aren't effeminate (or Fred cannot determine this from his vantage point). Fred assumes that the religious way he has elected to live his life is probably not shared by these two gay men. Fred fears God, he fears judgment, and his imaginary truth is that these two men should also.

Fred thinks about his young son witnessing this and then becoming gay as a result, and he grows fearful and angry. His reality is one of disgust and anger. It takes all of his willpower to keep from walking over to the bench and chastising—or even assaulting—the two men. Instead, he walks past them shaking his head, murmuring under his breath. He carries this anger throughout the day and to dinner, where his wife notices his foul mood. When he explains why he's upset, she, too, becomes upset at the gay people she's never seen or met because of the way "they" spoiled dinner. This experience feeds *her* hatred for gays, which will add to her judged data for future events.

Fred's path through the process was so fast and so emotionally loaded that he no longer even questions how he got here. For him, most events that involve homosexuality go from event to this distorted reality very quickly.

Re-act and You'll See the Same Play Again

When we go from event to reality as unconsciously and as quickly as Fred did, we could label that a "reaction." The word "react" when broken down to its core parts is "re-act," or act again. When an event happens, our brain wants to take a shortcut in the name of survival. The faster we can identify threats, the faster we can start fighting or fleeing. We access our data, connect it to a truth, and re-act the way we acted the last time something similar occurred, which usually leads to the same reality we got last time too. In essence, when we re-act, we'll see the same play again. If we don't like that play, we need to start replacing our data (have new experiences) and challenging the judgments we've attached to that factual data.

The speed with which this whole process occurs, from initial event to experienced reality, is less than a second. The process happens so quickly it *feels* automatic. While some who have mastered it can control the path (and hence, the reality), I suspect that the majority of us will be happy to just understand how to revisit the appropriate junction. Then we can take a different path instead of our "automatic" re-action. If we do it often enough, the path we want will become automatic for those types of events.

When you aren't happy with the outcome (reality) of an event, I encourage you to take a moment to fold a sheet of paper in half to make two columns. Label the left column "factual" and the right column "judged."

In the left column, describe the event the way a video camera would have recorded it. No judgment, just pure, unbiased observation. Make sure you don't use *any* descriptive adjectives or nouns. For example, don't write, "My son is living a life of sin." A video camera doesn't understand the concept of "sin." You need to describe the event or situation in a *completely non-emotional way.*

In the right column, list all of your judgments and history surrounding this event or one like it. Keep in mind that you are affected by other people's experiences, so don't limit your list to things that have only happened to you personally. If you've formed a judgment based on someone else's experience, list it. Dig deep here, this isn't easy. Start by identifying what aspects of the factual reality you have an issue with. Look for judged data. If your or your child's homosexuality is the issue, ask yourself questions like these:

- What aspect of homosexuality specifically causes me discomfort?
- Am I scared about HIV or AIDS?
- Am I worried about what the people at church, school, or work will think of my child or me? (If so, it might be worth the effort to examine the need for acceptance in general.)

The important thing is to really explore the data that your mind is working with and where it comes from. Take the time you need to get this done because 90 percent of the change you can affect happens right here at this stage.

Perspective

The late comedian George Carlin once joked that anyone driving slower than us is an idiot and anyone driving faster than us is a maniac. It's important to note, however, that the people we label maniacs likely think we're idiots, and the people we label idiots likely think we're maniacs. Everyone has a perspective, and this is a powerful truth because it frees us from thinking our perspective is the only one available to us. Abraham Lincoln wisely understood this when he said, "We can complain because rose bushes have thorns, or rejoice because thorn bushes have roses."

Finding the perspective that positively changes our reality can be challenging for some of us at times. It might help to consider that there could be a deeper truth—what I labeled "actual truth"—which leads to ultimate reality. This deeper truth might be found through spirituality, religion, long walks in a forest alone, staring into the night sky, or whatever else you do to rise above yourself and notice how small you are in the universe. Dr. Carl Sagan has a passage I often read to gain such perspective called "The Pale Blue Dot."[2] Whenever I read the passage, I get goose bumps. Suddenly the problems that seemed so big, my disagreements that seemed so important, my feuds that seemed so justified, all take a back seat in awe and wonder. That is a change in perspective. Not every event in our lives needs this type of perspective shift, but some are large or painful enough to warrant it.

We have been conditioned as human beings to think that *our* perspective is *the* perspective, that *our* truth is *the* truth. I find

---

[2] The licensing of Dr. Sagan's work is complicated so I was unable to put the passage in the book but use the search engine of your choice to search for "Pale Blue Dot" or check YouTube.

that religious folks struggle here the most. After perhaps a lifetime of being told that there is only one truth—one "right" way—and it's written down here in this book or spoken by this holy man, it's easy to see a world that doesn't fit into that viewpoint as "wrong" and very difficult to see anything outside of it as "right."

I am going to take some time in Chapter 7: Homosexuality and Religion to discuss the various perspectives in the Bible that are often selectively disregarded, especially when it comes to homosexuality. The goal is to widen our views about all of life and the beauty of the differences that make us all uniquely wonderful—something that only strengthens my personal belief in a higher power rather than weakening it.

Accepting the fact that we all have our own perspectives is the beginning of empathy. That's our next stop.

Chapter 2: Empathy and an Open Mind

"Empathy fuels connection; sympathy drives disconnection."

– Brené Brown

Of all the emotional skills that human beings possess, none will contribute more to peace, whether it be peace of mind or world peace, than empathy. Empathy is defined as "the psychological identification with or vicarious experiencing of the feelings, thoughts, or attitudes of another."[3] It is only in the identification of the experience others are having that we can begin to respond to them in the same way we would want to be treated under those circumstances.

The Golden Rule

In almost every religion and ethical tradition, some form of the Golden Rule appears. Possibly the earliest reference to reciprocity was 2040–1650 BC. Here are just a few notable examples:

- "Never impose on others what you would not choose for yourself." – Confucius (c. 500 BC)
- "Avoid doing what you would blame others for doing." – Thales (c. 624 BC – c. 546 BC)
- "Do not do to others that which angers you when they do it to you." – Isocrates (436–338 BC)
- "You shall not take vengeance or bear a grudge against your kinsfolk. Love your neighbor as yourself: I am the LORD." – Leviticus 19:18
- "Do to others what you want them to do to you. This is the meaning of the law of Moses and the teaching of the prophets." – Matthew 7:12
- "Do to others what you would want them to do to you." – Luke 6:31
- "Aheb li akheek ma tuhibu li nafsik." (Translation: "Wish for your brother, what you wish for yourself," or "Love your brother as you love yourself.") – Muhammad

---

[3] "Empathy," *The American Heritage® New Dictionary of Cultural Literacy,* 3rd ed. Houghton Mifflin Harcourt, 2005, accessed December 30, 2018, http://dictionary.reference.com/browse/empathy.

There are literally dozens more examples, and I think you get the idea. It's safe to say that the Golden Rule is one of the most common teachings across all of mankind from earliest recorded history. The Golden Rule is not enough, however. As Dr. Frank Crane put it, "The Golden Rule is of no use to you whatsoever unless you realize that it's your move." You are the one being urged to treat others the way you would want to be treated. To do this, we need the ability to control our ego and to develop our self-awareness.

Letting Go of the Ego

In order to treat others as we would like to be treated, it's helpful to truly understand another's situation. To do that, we use empathy. Empathy is the ability to imagine another's circumstances as if they were ours.

Empathy isn't just useful for the Golden Rule, it's useful for navigating life in general and is considered a cornerstone for emotional intelligence. Indeed, empathy is such an important part of normal societal interactions that a lack of empathy is considered one of the main indicators of sociopathic behavior.

Everywhere we look these days, we're seeing signs of violence, greed, and self-serving behavior. I would argue that these do not—in many cases—indicate a lack of empathy, however. Instead, I believe that we reject our empathetic impulses to justify our violations of the Golden Rule by telling ourselves a good story that lets us off the hook. "That guy begging for money would probably just use it for cigarettes." "That woman with the screaming kid is a terrible mom." "That person working at this fast food place should just go get an education." "This gay kid is insulting my gender with his behavior. He should just act like a man and stop disrespecting his family."

If we allowed ourselves to suspend these stories or see them for what they are, we'd allow our empathy to take root and that might explain why we don't *want* to do that. If we allow ourselves to really feel what the other is feeling, then our stories might be wrong, and our egos spend *a lot* of energy trying to be right.

Confirmation Bias

Confirmation bias (also called "my side bias") is one of the ego's defense mechanisms. It works like this:
1. We make an opinion or form a conclusion.
2. We search for, interpret, prefer, and recall information that confirms the opinion or conclusion.
3. We ignore, minimize, and explain away information that contradicts it.

It makes sense that the ego can step in to prevent empathy from taking hold. Empathy can break us from the trance our ego has cast upon us in an instant. Have you ever had the experience of watching someone you dislike go through something horrific and you suddenly see them in a new light, perhaps hate them a little less? If so, congratulations. You used empathy to triumph over ego.

One method to overcome the ego and get our empathy to come back online is to ask ourselves some questions. These questions are ones our egos will try to answer with stories, so we must fight to resist the urge to be "right" and instead strive to be accurate:
- What are the emotions this person might be going through? (If you don't have a clue, it may be because you aren't aware of your own feelings. See "Developing Self-Awareness" later in this chapter.)
- If I were this way or in this situation, how would I want to be treated? What would my challenges be? What would I need from others more than anything?
- Is my choice of feeling about the situation colored by my judgments or opinions? What would a video camera observe about this person or this situation, and how does that affect my reactions?

Once you've gone through this mental exercise, you may wish to further increase the accuracy of your assessment of the situation by asking the other person questions like:

- I'm wondering how you're feeling about this?
- What do you need from me more than anything right now? (I once asked a friend for advice and he replied, "Do you want my advice or my support? Because they aren't always the same thing." I've never forgotten that. Can *you* support someone on something that you advise against or disagree with?)
- If I were going through this, I'd feel _____. Is that how you're feeling?
- How have my actions been affecting you? What could I do differently?

Owning Feelings

Owning one's feelings is a very important way to remind everyone involved of the boundaries of responsibility, and it's also a key way to remind ourselves that we are the only ones who can control our feelings as we discussed in Chapter 1: Your Mind. Friend or Foe?

Owning your feelings means avoiding statements like "When you did that, *you made me* so mad." That makes you a victim to other people's actions, and it's a terrible way to live life. You are not a pinball to everyone else's bumpers. You get to choose what feelings you're going to have. A better way to phrase that might be "When you do that, I feel so angry." It's a subtle difference, but it acknowledges that no one "made you" feel anything.

Even when phrased the second way, we're so accustomed to being blamed for others' feelings that we tend to *hear* it the first way. This can cause a defensive response at first. It may take some time and gentle reminders that you're owning your feeling and not blaming the other for it. They did something, and you feel a certain way. Someone else who observed that same action might feel entirely different about it. If you continually work at this, you'll find communications are calmer and you'll feel more empowered to change how you feel about things.

Fighting Words

While we're discussing communication in this way, we should probably talk about two words that are the best fight starters in the English language: "always" and "never." No two words have started more fights than these two. If you want to start a fight, tell someone else that they "always" do something or "never" do something—and while you're at it, blame them for how you feel about it.

Good communication cannot occur while we're busy defending ourselves against the "always" and "never" attacks, nor can it happen when we're being blamed for someone else's feelings.

Developing Self-Awareness

You may be very willing to be empathic, but when you stare at another with empathic eyes, you see a blank slate. This might be because your ability to detect and describe your own feelings may be impaired. How can you possibly imagine how someone else would feel in a given circumstance if you cannot describe how *you* would feel in that circumstance?

For many of us, feelings are described very simply. We're either mad, glad, sad, or scared. This may seem easy, and yet there are actually a great number of nuanced emotions experienced by animals and humans. In an attempt to describe them, psychologist Robert Plutchik created the following "Wheel of Emotions" model in 1980:

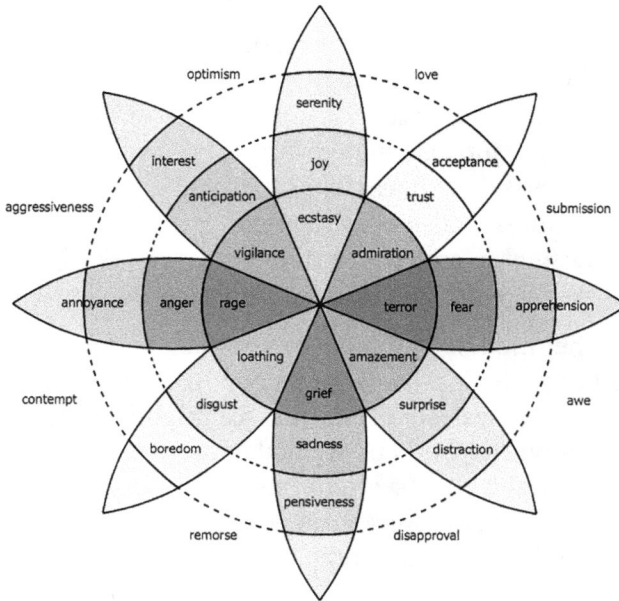

Figure 4: Wheel of Emotions[4]

A couple of interesting things about the model:

- Emotions are positioned in opposites on the model. Amazement is the opposite of vigilance, ecstasy is the opposite of grief, admiration is the opposite of loathing, and so on.
- The basic emotions (as Plutchik called them) actually appear on the first ring from the center of the chart. They are joy, trust, fear, surprise, sadness, disgust, anger, and anticipation.
- The emotions go from strongest to weakest as they move from the center to the outside, so rage is the strongest expression of the basic emotion of anger, and annoyance is the weakest.
- Plutchik believed that the basic emotions combine to make feelings that are indicated in between the various leaves of

---

[4] By Machine Elf 1735 (Own work) [Public domain], via Wikimedia Commons.

the model as follows:
- ○ Anticipation + joy = optimism
- ○ Joy + trust = love
- ○ Trust + fear = submission
- ○ Fear + surprise = awe
- ○ Surprise + sadness = disapproval
- ○ Sadness + disgust = remorse
- ○ Disgust + anger = contempt
- ○ Anger + anticipation = aggressiveness

There are other models with many more feeling words. I've attached a list of feeling words in Appendix A: Feeling Words.

There are a variety of reasons we might need help identifying emotions. Perhaps we had a traumatic experience that went along with the expression of emotion as a child, and we've learned to suppress emotions as an adult because it feels safer. Perhaps one or both of our parents punished or teased us for crying or dampened our joy with negativity. Perhaps we told someone how we felt and they rejected us. If these kinds of experiences happened to you, you may have learned to compensate by becoming numb to emotion in your life. I know someone who was so uncomfortable with feelings that he once said if there were a pill to permanently eliminate emotion, he'd take it.

If you find it difficult to identify your emotions, you may want to focus there before trying your hand at empathy. One way to improve is to stop from time to time throughout the day and ask yourself, "How do I feel right now?" and then use Appendix A: Feeling Words to identify some that seem to fit. There is no right or wrong here. The purpose is to hone your skills at listening to your body. Over time, this will become more automatic and require less concentration. You will start building a database in your mind of events and physical sensations and then matching them to their resulting feelings. You can then use this to begin practicing empathy with others.

You don't even need to have real experiences to practice empathy. You can practice just using your imagination. Here are some examples to try:

- You are standing on a street corner and observe a homeless man ask a passerby, "Can you please spare anything to help me eat today?" The person sneers back, "Get a job!" and walks on. The homeless man looks down at the ground and frowns.
  - Exercise: What kinds of feelings do you think the homeless man is feeling? What about the passerby? Try to put yourself in each of their places.
- Your boss announces that he's going to stop holding the team accountable for their work as a group and begin holding team members accountable individually instead.
  - Exercise: What kind of behavior do you think this will drive with the team? What do you think each team member might feel? How would a high performer feel? A low performer? Why might the boss think this is the right decision?
- Your son is the pitcher on the softball team. The score is tied in the ninth inning, and he pitches a ball that is hit way over the outfielders' heads, resulting in a game-winning home run for the other team.
  - Exercise: How do you think your son feels before that pitch? While the ball is in the air? After it lands? What factors might come into play that will affect your son's feelings after the game is over and the team is gathering in the dugout?
- Your daughter just found out that the person she likes at school asked a different girl out to the prom.
  - Exercise: What do you think she's going through? How will her actions or words perhaps betray her true feelings? What might she need from you?

Regardless of our religious background or lack thereof, the ubiquitous nature of the Golden Rule suggests that it is a universal human goal to proactively treat others as one desires to be treated. Without empathy, it's difficult to imagine how our actions feel to someone else, and that makes it difficult to follow the Golden Rule. Now that you have your empathy muscles toned, it's time to start challenging your feelings around homosexuality.

Part Two: Homosexuality Basics

"I don't think that you can write music if you don't know how to play an instrument. You have to know the basics, then you can go forward."

— Alber Elbaz

Chapter 3: Stereotypes and Myths

"Yeah, I had gay friends. The first thing I realized was that everybody's different, and it becomes obvious that all of the gay stereotypes are ridiculous."

– Bruce Springsteen

When I was a teenage boy, Phil Donahue was the king of daytime television. He was the "Oprah" of my childhood. From time to time, he would have gay men on the show to discuss gay rights issues, and, the way I remember it, they would almost always be very effeminate men. At the time, I thought that's what it meant to be gay. Since I wasn't effeminate, I reasoned, I must not be gay. As I mentioned earlier, I'd had sexual experiences with boys from age five all the way into my teens, but I wrote them off as a phase I'd yet to grow out of. I carried this belief with me into my early twenties—even though I was sleeping with men the whole time. The media certainly didn't help. Gay men, when they were portrayed at all, were usually effeminate or sexually deviant. I was masculine, and nothing about my sexual activities seemed "deviant."

The moment I decided to come out, I told myself that even if I was the only non-effeminate gay man on the planet, I was gay. I decided that coming out and acknowledging that I was gay would at least protect me from bigots. I reasoned that if they knew I was gay, they'd be more likely to keep their opinions to themselves while I was around. What I wasn't counting on was that my coming out would actually change their opinions.

My life since then has been one opportunity after another to dispel the most common stereotypes that many of the straight people I meet seem to have. All stereotypes are based upon some truth because, by nature, they're based on amalgams of real people. It's just important to note that a majority of these populations do not fit into those stereotypes and usually blend in with the rest of the population so well that their membership into their segment is not noticed.

The problem with stereotypes in general is that they oversimplify the reality. It is human nature to want things to be simple because we are evolutionarily driven to judge quickly. After all, the difference between life and death would historically depend on our correctly judging the rustling in the bushes as a lion preparing to pounce. Judging is much faster if we can make things fit into as few boxes (patterns) as necessary. It's much easier for us to judge gays as bad if we can take one aspect of how some gay people show up, that we feel uncomfortable with, and turn it into a belief that all gay people are like that.

The difference with homosexual stereotypes is that we don't have a physical characteristic that puts us into the segment called "gay." We might be able to identify black and Asian people by their skin color, but there are gay black and Asian people. There is not one single physical characteristic that can be attributed to being gay.

I match almost none of the stereotypes associated with being gay, so people often are quite surprised when I tell them. I often have to "out" myself more frequently than someone who might better fit the stereotype, and I do this because I want to save the other person from embarrassment should any homophobia they might have lurch out of their mouths during one of our conversations.

I learned this lesson in my late twenties. I had just joined a new fitness club, and along with the membership came a complimentary hour with a fitness trainer. I was assigned an attractive young man who started touring the club with me and getting me started on the various machines. During each stop, this man felt it necessary to point out the derriere of every female within thirty feet. He was obviously in heat. After about the tenth time I was tiring of it, so I said to him with a giggle, "Hey, just so you know, I'm gay, so I'm not appreciating these butts nearly as much as you are."

"Why do you people always have to tell everybody you're gay? Why can't you just keep it to yourself?" he exclaimed. I pointed out that he'd been telling me how straight he was for the past forty-five minutes. Gym membership: $145. Blank expression on the homophobic trainer's face: priceless.

My experience shows that much of the acceptance of homosexuality seems hampered by these stereotypes. If you're a gay person, you may even be holding some of them against yourself. It is completely possible (and some psychologists might argue, common) for gay people to have a bit of homophobia themselves. When we're raised in a world that either paints homosexuality negatively or is silent about the matter, the only messages we receive are the negative ones. Sports stars come out after they retire. Actors come out in the twilight of their careers. We quickly learn that being gay isn't to be discussed and that if we are homosexual, there is something "wrong" with us. It's a small step to take these judgments and make them internal. Stereotypes just make it easier.

I want to dispel a few of these stereotypes in the coming pages, but I don't want you to mistake my explanations for judgement. When I say, for example, that not all gay men are effeminate, by no means am I inferring that there is anything wrong with being effeminate. I'm merely observing that not all gays are this way. The goal here is to bring some light to these black and white statements so that we can all agree that there are quite a few shades of gray in between. I will also freely admit that much of my evidence against these stereotypes and myths comes from personal experience and thus is subjective. I'm OK with this because personal experience is what dispels all stereotypes. Therefore, if you have a strong stereotype against a given population or don't believe what I tell you about these myths, I encourage you to get to know some members of that population and let your personal experience guide you to the truth. This is true whether you're struggling with racism, homophobia, misogyny, or any other oversimplification of a segment of the population.

Myth 1: Being Gay Is a Choice

"There are about 642 species of animal that exhibit homosexual activity, but you know there is only one species that exhibits homophobia, and that's mankind. So, who's natural?" – Stephen Fry

This is the mother of all myths about homosexuality. The opposition to gay rights and acceptance of and empathy towards gays all seem to revolve around this one myth. I can promise you that if it were a choice to be black, black people would still be fighting for the right to vote and marry interracially because white people would just tell black people, hey, if you want to vote or get married, be white.

As I mentioned, I've been attracted to males since I was five years old. That may seem a bit "out there" to some, but it's true. I've never once slept with a woman and have never had the desire to do so, and I'm not alone. Many gay people I've known in my life have understood that they were gay from a very early age. The only choice they've felt in the matter was whether to be honest about it or not.

There is ongoing research to find the "gay gene," and even if it's found, some will still continue to believe it's a choice. The most recent theories about homosexuality's roots are pointing, at least in part, to the field of epigenetics. Epigenetics is the study of changes to DNA made by external influences while the fetus is developing, like switches that can toggle this way or that, depending on influences unique to the mother. Recent studies have looked at the statistical curiosity that the more offspring a mother has had, the more likely she will give birth to a gay child. Studies are ongoing and still inconclusive as I write this, but epigenetics would certainly explain the mechanism by which nature would accomplish this. It would make sense evolutionarily as well if the evolutionary "purpose" of homosexuality in nature is population control. This is especially true as newborns are born into famine or resource-starved environments.

Those who believe that homosexuality is a choice tend to believe that it's "unnatural." The word *unnatural* means "that which goes against nature." Homosexual behavior has been documented in over fifteen hundred species,[5] so it's a bit of a misnomer to call homosexuality unnatural. But let's assume that by unnatural, these people are not talking about nature and instead are talking about what is "normal"—a term that is so subjective, I'm forced to put it in quotes.

Indulge me for a moment and let me guide you on a little exercise about what's normal. Please clasp your hands together by interlocking your fingers. Rest your hands together in front of

---

[5] "1,500 Animal Species Practice Homosexuality," News-Medical.net, October 23, 2006, web.archive.org/web/20070929131358/http://www.news-medical.net/?id=20718..

you. Feel normal? Which thumb is on top, your left or your right? Now switch thumbs. Feels strange, doesn't it? For about half the people asked to do this, that is the thumb that is on top for them and it feels entirely unnatural to have it your initial way, so what is natural for one person is often unnatural for another. Don't take my word for it, though, go ahead and try this out with friends and family. What made you put your hands in the initial configuration? When did you choose which thumb to place on top? Being gay feels just like that for me: completely natural, and there was never a decision for me to be that way.

If you happen to be straight, when did you choose to be that way? If this were a choice, it would certainly be a big, memorable one, wouldn't it? Think about what a person would be choosing between: fit in with everyone by being "normal" *or* be the subject of jokes, get teased in school, get disowned by the family and get kicked out of the house, potentially give up having kids and continuing the family name, limit career choices and where one can live, and lose friends. Does that sound like a decision you'd make lightly or one you'd stand behind when suffering these consequences?

You might be thinking that bisexual people are choosing. After all, they're equally attracted (in all forms of attraction) to both genders. Please don't confuse the ability to choose which gender they want to spend their lives with as choosing their sexuality. They can choose which gender they want to date, *but they cannot choose not to have that choice.*

I've heard some argue that women seem to be more able to choose their sexuality than men. I stand my ground, however, on my belief that these women are merely more able to freely express their natural sexuality because society accepts this gradation in women more than with men. My belief is that if society accepted homosexuality in men the way that it accepts it in women, we'd see more men exploring their natural sexuality than forcing themselves to play the role of a straight person simply because that's the "manly" thing to do.

Myth 2: All Gay Men Are Effeminate/All Lesbians Are Masculine

I won't lie. I get a lot of enjoyment out of shattering this one to pieces on an almost daily basis. Most people tell me they had *no idea* I was gay until I told them. This is both a blessing and a curse. It means I have to come out again and again—*a lot.* Every time I change jobs or meet new friends.

Just like sexual orientation is not binary, so too degree of masculinity/femininity, gender identity, and even gender itself are not. I can have male body parts and still feel like a woman, or vice versa. Even though Mother Nature appears to be mostly binary with regards to gender in humans, there are children born with both sexual organs. This is increasingly being accepted in the medical community as a normal (if rare) biological development in humans.

It's beyond the scope of this book to dive deeply into gender and the expression of it, but the main takeaway is that there are boys who, from an early age, express themselves with feminine energy and girls who do so with masculine energy (tomboys). This behavior is completely separate from their sexual orientation in many cases.

Effeminate gay males are more vulnerable to bullying in the suburbs because it's difficult for them to blend in. They feel safer in larger numbers, so they tend to gravitate to major metropolitan gay neighborhoods when they mature into adults. This was especially true when I was growing up. In the parts of the world that are becoming more gay friendly, gay neighborhoods are becoming less common.

This variety of expressions of masculinity and femininity make sense if you really stop and think about it. Don't you know straight men who are really "manly" and some who are very "sensitive"? Don't you know straight women who do the home improvement work and straight men who seem to have a touch for decorating? If this range of expression exists for straight people, it certainly does for gay people as well.

Again, I want to reiterate that there is nothing wrong with effeminate males or masculine females. If you or someone you know fit these descriptions, what I hope you get from this myth is that the spectrum of masculinity and femininity in humans is vast and it is separate from whom we're attracted to.

Myth 3: Gay People Are Easy to Spot

This myth goes hand in hand with Myth 2. Because people think all gay people behave a certain way, many people believe that we're easy to spot. By extension, they also believe we all do certain professions. Gay men are supposedly all performing typically feminine careers such as interior decorator, hairdresser, and massage therapist, while lesbians typically perform masculine careers such as police officer, firefighter, and construction worker. In truth, there are straight male interior decorators and gay male football players. There are lesbians who are makeup artists and hairdressers.

My personal experience provides me many examples that this stereotype is wrong. I had a good friend growing up who's straight and has way better taste with colors and interior design decisions than I do. I went to high school with a guy who is the poster child for straightness. He's a very successful interior decorator now with a child and is married to a woman. I know several closeted firefighters who are gay (it's very tough for firefighters to come out due to their close living quarters). There are, of course, thousands of gay people serving in the military who, until recently, were under constant fear of being outed, then ousted. I can promise you that if we lined them all up in a row, you would have a difficult time picking out which ones were gay.

This brings up a huge pet peeve of mine. It makes my blood boil when people refer to something called the "gay lifestyle." Rock stars have a *lifestyle*. Gay people have *lives*, and they aren't that different from the lives of straight people. There are gay firefighters, police officers, garbage collectors, professional football players, hair stylists, interior decorators, landscapers, and accountants, and they do not all share a similar lifestyle.

Myth 4: Gay Men Are Attracted to All Men

If I said that all straight men were attracted to all women, you'd call bullshit, but if I said that all gay men are attracted to all men, some people would believe that. It defies logic to assume that straight men have preferences and attractions to specific types of women but gay men just have belt buckles hitting the floor when we get in proximity of other males. There is nothing about being gay that changes anything about being male. We are just as selective or nonselective as we would have been as males, regardless of our orientation.

There can be a bit of a pent-up feeling after being in the closet for years. Since we're suddenly liberated and can seek out other men more openly, some men do that with more reckless abandon than others. And there are gay men who are attracted to straight men in a sort of forbidden fruit kind of way, but that is still not *all* straight men. Just men who meet their definition of handsome.

There is no reason for straight men to fear gay men. If you're a straight man and tend to attract gay men to you, it's likely a compliment, and most gay men will take a polite "I'm straight" in stride. We're statistically used to hearing it. As a famous "straight guy" Internet meme goes, "Say something nice about gay guys. Not only do they leave more girls for us, they take another dude with them."

Myth 5: AIDS Is God's Punishment for Homosexuals

I have a bit of personal experience with this myth because my uncle (rest his soul) once told me this before I came out of the closet. What's particularly nasty about this one is that neither side can prove or disprove the other. Since both sides are trying to speak for God, all we have to go by is the teachings of the Bible and, more specifically, of Jesus. Christian faiths claim to follow the teachings of Jesus Christ. According to the Bible, Jesus never mentions homosexuality once, so I find it difficult to believe that He would condone a deadly disease for anyone, never mind homosexuals.

I'm baffled by a belief in the kind of vengeful God that would need to exist for this myth to be true. I believe in a God who is a bit more secure than one who would punish an entire class of humans because He doesn't approve of the way He made them. It seems incongruous to me that God can be so powerful that He can create a disease to punish gay people but not powerful enough to prevent them from being gay in the first place.

Moreover, it's important to note that HIV, as a sexually transmitted disease, knows no boundary for gender or sexual orientation. The spread of HIV requires direct exposure to an infected person's bodily fluid. The bodily fluid that contains the highest concentration is blood, followed by semen (including precum), then vaginal secretions, then breast milk. During intercourse (both vaginal and anal), small, invisible tears can occur in either partner. If small amounts of fluid from the infected person come into contact with those tears, the risk of infection goes up. The sexual practices that increase the probability of that transfer are dry vaginal intercourse and anal intercourse. (Oral intercourse is not without risk but is considered low risk because the virus can't survive well in the mouth.)

Assuming HIV spreads in only one sexual orientation gives a dangerous false sense of security, which only perpetuates the disease further. HIV is a contact-spread virus, and that contact is happening all around the world by people of all different sexual orientations.

Myth 6: Gay Parents Raise Gay Children

Those who believe this also believe that being gay is a choice. In their minds, a gay couple can and will raise a child to be gay. I would argue that if you asked my parents (both straight) if they chose to raise me gay, they'd say no. Yet here I am, gay as can be. If two gay people can make a child gay, shouldn't a straight couple be able to make a child straight? Since likely 99 percent of gay children are born to straight couples, what is going on in all these straight households that's making us all gay? The answer, of course, is nothing. Human sexuality is not believed to be affected in either direction by nurturing (or even lack of nurturing). What *is* affected is the *acceptance* of the sexuality we were born with.

In my experience, children raised by gay couples are likely to be a lot more secure about their sexuality, whatever it is. Having had to face down judgment and prejudice by a society that seems to enjoy the sport of bullying, they will tend to be less judgmental, less prejudicial, and more comfortable with expressing themselves. As a result, if by chance a child raised by a gay couple were gay, they'd likely come out sooner and with more confidence than a child raised by a straight couple who raised that child without this tolerance to differences. This could lead people to believe that there are more gay kids of gay parents when in fact there are just more openly gay kids in that situation.

As an aside, I've also heard that gay people shouldn't raise children because of the bullying that child may get growing up from peers. Not to point out the obvious here, but that bullying is coming from society. How about we focus our concern and energy on those who bully these kids rather than prevent them from having parents who love them?

Myth 7: It's Just a Phase

I actually bought into this one myself for a while when I was younger. It kept me in the closet much longer than I probably would have been otherwise. All the while I was sleeping with friends and falling deeply in love with them, I was in denial telling myself that I'd yet to outgrow that preadolescent phase where girls have cooties and interest in the same sex is common.

By the time I'd turned twenty-two, it was getting a bit hard to deny, but deny I did. Sexuality is a process of discovery, not deciding. Expression of that sexuality is dependent upon many, many factors including how safe we feel with being honest about it with our friends and family. The funny thing about this myth is we have no idea where it came from. You'd think that there were large masses of people in the world who were gay for a while then suddenly just decided they were straight instead. But those masses do not exist. Coming out of the closet is usually a one-way trip for most gay people. Even those who go back in have not changed their orientation—they just become less open/resume lying about it again.

Myth 8: Strong/Weak Parenting or Childhood Trauma Causes Homosexuality

If this myth were true, it would be so easy to predict homosexuality. It's just not this simple. It's estimated that about 3 percent of the population has some level of homosexuality, which means that there are approximately 222 million people alive right now who are partially or entirely gay as you are reading this sentence. The assertion that all of these people had parenting issues or traumatic experiences as children would be very easy to prove if it were true—and people have tried unsuccessfully. The fact is, there are many gay people who are born into very loving, supportive families and who have never experienced trauma and many, many straight people born into abusive families who *have* experienced childhood trauma. Each of those would not be possible if this myth were true.

This myth stems from some work in 1920 by Dr. Sigmund Freud. Psychology was a very young field in 1920, and in the years since his death in 1939, we've learned much about the human mind that has disproven much of Freud's work, notably his theories around strong mothers and weak fathers affecting the sexuality of children. According to George Dvorsky:[6]

> Virtually no institution in any discipline would dare use [Freud] as a credible source. In 1996, *Psychological Science* reached the conclusion that "[T]here is literally nothing to be said, scientifically or therapeutically, to the advantage of the entire Freudian system or any of its component dogmas." As a research paradigm, it's pretty much dead.

---

[6] George Dvorsky, "Why Freud Still Matters, When He Was Wrong About Almost Everything," editorial, Io9.com. Gawker Media, August 7, 2013, https://io9.gizmodo.com/why-freud-still-matters-when-he-was-wrong-about-almost-1055800815#.

Needless to say, a boy with a strong, dominating mother and/or a weak father is not more likely to be gay than one with those dispositions reversed. The strength and weakness of parents *does* influence how safe a child feels about coming out, but more about that in Chapter 8: So, You Have a Gay Child.

Myth 9: Gays Should Just Keep It to Themselves

Whether you yourself are gay or have a gay son or daughter, you may be asking yourself, "Why come out at all?" The reasoning goes like this: People don't walk around talking about how straight they are, why do gays have to walk around talking about how gay they are? Wouldn't it be much easier if everyone just kept their business to themselves?

The thing is, people *do* talk about how straight they are every day. Every time you hear Sarah at work say, "My boyfriend and I went hiking over the weekend," Sarah is telling you she's straight. When Sarah's boyfriend joins the two of you for lunch that day and they hold hands during the walk to the restaurant, they are telling the world that they are straight. The billboard above you on the street that shows a man and a woman holding hands on the beach tells you that advertising agencies think you're straight. Sarah doesn't have to tell you what sexual positions she enjoys with her boyfriend for you to know her orientation. She doesn't have to discuss her sex life at all.

The concept of "keeping our business to ourselves" can mean a lot of things. If we define "business" as the intimate details of our sex lives, that's probably not the kind of thing we should be discussing or demonstrating around strangers, straight or gay. If "business" means who I love, who I share a home with, or who I spent last weekend with, it becomes pretty difficult to defend wanting to silence that.

Closeted gay people have to police their pronouns—Steve is careful to replace "he" with "she" when he's talking about his date with Jeff. He's forced to reduce Jeff to a "friend" when introducing the man he's lived with for two years. Steve loves Jeff the same way Sarah loves her boyfriend, yet, to remain closeted, he cannot do what Sarah does: share that love with the rest of us. Even gays who are out of the closet will sometimes avoid the topic if we don't know someone's politics. It's just easier not to bring it up sometimes.

If you want to understand what this is like, try to do it for a day. Just go around and try not to mention the name of your husband (if you're a straight woman) or wife (if you're a straight man). Try not to even use the correct pronoun. See if the stress of it all just makes you shut down socially. While all your coworkers are sharing stories about their weekend, you'll be deciding that the excitement of sharing yours isn't worth the risk of slipping up, so you'll sit there and smile—at least on the outside.

Myth 10: Homosexuals Are Pedophiles

Some years ago, I was participating in a program that aimed to bring gay men and women to high school and college human sexuality classes. The format was simple. We (usually a one-man and one-woman pair) would take about five to ten minutes each to tell the class about ourselves, and then we'd open it up for any question. We wanted the kids to feel comfortable asking any question they had, so we encouraged them to err on the side of asking, and if we felt uncomfortable with the question, we'd tell them.

At one particular session, the lesbian woman I was speaking with told the class that she was a mother of three school-aged kids and explained that her days looked a lot like their parents' days: bringing kids to softball and dance classes, fixing meals, cleaning house, coaching a team, and working full-time. When she was finished, one of the first questions we got was from a girl in the class. She asked, "With all the activities you have going on and with how busy you are, how do you find time to molest kids?" I remember briefly thinking that the girl was joking, but the look on her face was neutral and curious. This was a genuine belief of hers—I'm assuming planted in her head at home.

My speaking partner didn't miss a beat. She explained that homosexuality and pedophilia are not the same thing, and she was glad to have the opportunity to explain that to the girl that day.

As a scientific aside, the term "pedophilia" means a sexual attraction to prepubescent children. Once a child begins puberty, they are biologically known as adolescents. Those with an attraction to adolescents are called "hebephiles." I will not make the distinction here since the research is the same for both.

Professor Gregory M. Herek points out in a University of California, Davis study called "Facts About Homosexuality and Child Molestation" that accusing disliked minority groups of these types of activities is common:

> "Members of disliked minority groups are often stereotyped as representing a danger to the majority's most vulnerable members. For example, Jews in the Middle Ages were accused of murdering Christian babies in ritual sacrifices. Black men in the United States were often lynched after being falsely accused of raping white women. In a similar fashion, gay people have often been portrayed as a threat to children. [7]

The most important thing to note about pedophilia is that it describes an *age-based* sexual attraction rather than a *gender-based* attraction. Referring to abuse of male children by adult males as "homosexual molestation" and abuse of female children by adult males as "heterosexual molestation" is imprecise because it presumes that the orientation of the perpetrator is what is being referred to. Most male molesters of boys do not report sexual interest in adult men (Herek).

The conversation isn't one of orientation but of age. Herek writes:

> "[M]any child molesters *don't have an adult sexual orientation.* They have never developed the capacity for mature sexual relationships with other adults, either men or women. Instead their sexual attractions focus on children—boys, girls, or children of both sexes." (Herek, emphasis added)

---

[7] Gregory M. Herek, "Facts about Homosexuality and Child Molestation," *Sexual Orientation: Science, Education, and Policy*, University of California, Davis, accessed December 30, 2018, https://psychology.ucdavis.edu/rainbow/html/facts_molestation.html.

In 1978, a study was conducted of 175 adult males who were convicted of sexual assault against a child. None of the men had an exclusively homosexual adult orientation. In 1994:

> Dr. Carole Jenny and her colleagues reviewed 352 medical charts, representing all of the sexually abused children seen in the emergency room or child abuse clinic of a Denver children's hospital during a one-year period. The molester was a gay or lesbian adult in fewer than 1 percent of cases in which an adult molester could be identified—only 2 of the 269 cases. (Herek)

The study concludes:

> The empirical research does not show that gay or bisexual men are any more likely than heterosexual men to molest children. This is not to argue that homosexual and bisexual men never molest children. But there is no scientific basis for asserting that they are more likely than heterosexual men to do so. And, as explained above, many child molesters cannot be characterized as having an adult sexual orientation at all; they are fixated on children (Herek)

Experience Is Your Teacher

If you believed any of the stereotypes we just explored (or find my explanations to be unconvincing), I strongly recommend that you go out and meet some gay people. Perhaps attend a Parents and Friends of Lesbian and Gays (PFLAG) meeting in your area. Doing so will provide you with more data and will help you choose factual data instead of judged data. I won't promise you that you won't meet some people who fit some of these stereotypes—all stereotypes are loosely based upon some portion of the population—but the exercise will be very useful to help you see that they do not apply across the board, and you'll meet some great people in the process!

Humans are pattern-matching machines. Stereotypes help our brains to shortcut critical thought. When we were cavemen and cavewomen, that was a survival advantage. It doesn't serve us in modern times the same way. Challenging these stereotypes is an important step in re-engaging your critical thinking skills. It will benefit you greatly in the material yet to come

Chapter 4: What Does It Mean to Be Gay?

"My own belief is that there is hardly anyone whose sexual life, if it were broadcast, would not fill the world at large with surprise and horror."

— W. Somerset Maugham

I do not have as one of my aims to help you settle the question of whether you are gay or straight or something in between, but there is some validity in at least exploring what it means to be gay. The clinical definition of homosexuality is "a person sexually attracted to persons of the same sex."[8] While I think being homosexual is even more than this, I think the best way to approach what it means to be gay is to first discuss what it isn't. It isn't where you live, what you do for a living, how you talk, what you wear, what kind of car you drive, or whom you hang out with. It isn't even who you sleep with. You may be thinking, "Wait a minute. I was with you until that statement. Come on! Isn't sleeping with the same gender the very essence of being gay?"

It may surprise you to know that there is actually a subset of men who desire sex with men—even into their adult years—but identify as straight. Typically, they enjoy long, committed romantic and sexual relations with women but crave sex with men also. Dr. Joe Kort has done some very good work in this area. He wrote the book *Is My Husband Gay, Straight, or Bi?: A Guide for Women Concerned about Their Men* and holds seminars for men (and in many cases, their wives) who are trying to understand this behavior. Dr. Kort would argue that most of these men are straight—despite their desire to have sex with other men.

Sleeping with the same gender does not, in itself, make someone gay. Sex, at its core, is simply heat and friction (admittedly not good sex, but that's a different book). My own personal experience confirms this. I slept with quite a few boys my age when I was in junior high and high school that are now happily married with kids. Just because they slept with me then doesn't mean they were or are gay. Even the fact that I slept with them didn't, alone, make *me* gay. This works both ways, by the way. A gay man is no straighter simply because he sleeps with a

---

[8] "Medical Definition of *Homosexual*," MedicineNet.com, December 12, 2018, http://www.medterms.com/script/main/art.asp?articlekey=3781.

woman. Our sexual identity is much more complicated and fascinating than who we lie down next to on a given evening.

So, what's missing? What magic dust gets sprinkled into the mix to make someone gay? In a word, love. What defines my sexual identity is not just who I sleep with, but who I fall in love with combined with who I find sexually attractive. Love is the component that's missing in the same-sex experiences of the straight men that Dr. Kort studies, and, in my case, it's what differentiated me from my classmates in my teenage years. I used to say if my pubescent years had a theme song, it would be "I Can't Make You Love Me" by Bonnie Raitt. What finally convinced me I was gay wasn't just that I was sleeping with other males; it was that I fell in love with them.

A Spectrum of Sexuality

Dr. Alfred Kinsey conducted exhaustive clinical research on the topic of human sexuality. To complete the work, Kinsey interviewed roughly 6,300 men about their sexuality. His research led him to publish a book called *Sexual Behavior in the Human Male* in 1948. In the sections of the work dedicated to sexual orientation, Kinsey was quoted as saying:

> "Males do not represent two discrete populations, heterosexual and homosexual. The world is not to be divided into sheep and goats. It is a fundamental of taxonomy that nature rarely deals with discrete categories. [...] The living world is a continuum in each and every one of its aspects. While emphasizing the continuity of the gradations between exclusively heterosexual and exclusively homosexual histories, it has seemed desirable to develop some sort of classification, which could be based on the relative amounts of heterosexual and homosexual experience or response in each history. [...] An individual may be assigned a position on this scale, for each period in his life. [...] A seven-point scale comes nearer to showing the many gradations that actually exist (pp. 639, 656)."[9]

This scale is now famously known as the Kinsey scale, and you may have heard someone say, "I'm a Kinsey 4," or "I'm a Kinsey

---

[9] Alfred C. Kinsey, Wardell B. Pomeroy, and Clyde E. Martin, *Sexual Behavior in the Human Male* (Bloomington: Indiana University Press, 1948).

3." Kinsey believed that human sexual attraction fell on a seven-point scale from 0 to 6. Zero was entirely heterosexual and six was entirely homosexual with three neatly fitting in the middle as bisexual (an equal attraction to both genders).

Kinsey reported that nearly 46 percent of the male subjects had "reacted" sexually to persons of both sexes in the course of their adult lives, and 37 percent had at least one homosexual experience (p. 656). The number can also change as we age. 11.6 percent of white males aged twenty to thirty-five were given a rating of 3 for this period of their lives (Table 147, p. 651).

In 1993, Dr. Fritz Klein published *The Bisexual Option*. In it, he expanded on the Kinsey scale by adding three different time spans. His version is entitled "The Klein Grid," and is reproduced in Table 1 below:[10]

	Past (entire life up until a year ago)	Past (last 12 months)	Ideal (what would you like?)
A) Sexual Attraction: To whom are you sexually attracted?			
B) Sexual Behavior: With whom have you actually had sex?			
C) Sexual Fantasies: About whom are your sexual fantasies?			
D) Emotional Preference: Who do you feel more drawn to or close to emotionally?			

---

[10] Fritz Klein, "The Klein Sexuality Grid," American Institute of Bisexuality, 2014, accessed December 30, 2018, http://www.americaninstituteofbisexuality.org/thekleingrid/.

	Past (entire life up until a year ago)	Past (last 12 months)	Ideal (what would you like?)
E) Social Preference: Which gender do you socialize with?			
F) Lifestyle Preference: In which community do you like to spend your time? In which do you feel most comfortable?			
G) Self Identification: How do you label yourself?			

Each of the 21 boxes should contain a value from 1 to 7, categorizing the individual's answers to the questions. For variables A to E, the possible answers are: 1=Other sex only, 2=Other sex mostly, 3=Other sex somewhat more, 4=Both sexes, 5=Same sex somewhat more, 6=Same sex mostly, and 7=Same sex only. For variables F and G, these range from 1=Heterosexual only to 7=Homosexual only.

Table 1

Throughout all of these clinical studies and discussions, the word "attraction" is bantered about quite a bit, and I think it's important that we pause here for just a moment and discuss the word. As some of these studies infer, attraction is more than physical. Though physical attraction is a big part of it, let's not let it steal the show from all the other kinds of attractions, like spiritual attraction, intellectual attraction, emotional attraction, cultural attraction, and masculine/feminine attraction. There's even olfactory attraction (attraction through smell) where studies have shown that gay men are attracted to the smell of males as are heterosexual women, and lesbians are attracted to the smell of females as are heterosexual men.[11] All of these types of attractions combine to bring us physically closer to the people we want in our lives and farther from those we don't.

As I said, my hope for you is that regardless of where you believe you fall on the Kinsey scale or on the Klein Grid, after we're finished together, you'll feel better about who you or someone you love is. If you find yourself confused about your sexuality, I strongly recommend that you seek a professional who can help you dig a bit deeper as to why you may be cloudy. Most credentialed professional counselors and therapists are completely neutral about whether or not you're gay, and my advice is that you confirm this before starting your sessions. If they have biases against homosexuality, they're ignoring their profession's main diagnostic manual, which removed homosexuality as a mental disorder in 1973. You're there to get help figuring out who you are, not to get help becoming who they (or someone sending you there) might want you to be.

It is my firm belief—and it has been confirmed with a study by the American Psychological Association (see "Gay Reparative Therapy" in Chapter 8: So, You Have a Gay Child)—that our sexuality is what it is and there is no amount of "rehabilitation" which will make us one way or the other. We can rehabilitate behaviors but not who we are. As I said earlier, our sexuality is a process of discovery, not a process of becoming.

---

[11] Jessica D. Payne, "What Can Body Odor Tell Us about Sexual Attraction and Sexual Orientation," *The Observer*, April 14, 2010, ndsmcobserver.com/2010/04/what-can-body-odor-tells-us-about-sexual-attraction-and-sexual-orientation/.

Chapter 5: Homosexuality and the Media

"The media has changed. We now give broadcast licenses to philosophies instead of people. People get confused and think there is no difference between news and entertainment. People who project themselves as journalists on television don't know the first thing about journalism. They are just there stirring up a hockey game."

– Gary Ackerman

"If people in the media cannot decide whether they are in the business of reporting news or manufacturing propaganda, it is all the more important that the public understand that difference and choose their news sources accordingly."

– Thomas Sowell

When I first came out of the closet in the early 1990s, I was attending my first gay pride parade in San Francisco. From where I sat on the curbside, I was right in front of a cameraman from a major network as he was taking footage for the evening news. Every time a church group, an AIDS charity, or a group like Parents and Friends of Lesbians and Gays (PFLAG) went by, the camera would go down. If a naked sixty-five-year-old man on a bike or some woman with her boobs hanging out came by, he picked the camera up and filmed intently. I said to him as he walked in front of me, "Please tell me you're going to film some of these normal, everyday groups of people as well." He said, "I think I'll go find Reverend Phelps. He's normal," and then walked off.

The now-deceased "Reverend" Phelps created a website entitled godhatesfags.com. He and his followers—primarily family raised on his compound—routinely protest funerals of gay people and military personnel, saying that they are the reason for God's wrath on the planet.

This cameraman—all by himself, no producer, no director, no corporate media policy—was deciding what tens of thousands of viewers were going to see on the evening news that night . . . and his reference to Phelps indicated that he was homophobic, yet here he was: assigned to cover one of the most famous gay events in the world. It makes you wonder how many decisions like this are made in media every day.

The media is increasingly blurring the line between opinion and news. The days of Walter Cronkite coming on the screen with "Editorial" appearing in big letters while he gave his or the station's opinion are over. Now we're left to sort out who is presenting facts and who is presenting opinion from minute to minute. This is a very dangerous development during the Information Age, when information is pummeling us constantly. It is more important than it's ever been for us to take responsibility for fact-checking the information we receive before we form opinions—especially when those opinions affect the lives and freedoms of others.

Confirmation Bias

As we discussed in Chapter 2: Empathy and an Open Mind, there is a concept in psychology called confirmation bias, which basically means that we are naturally inclined to favor information that confirms beliefs we already hold over information that disproves it. It turns out that this has evolutionary purposes. According to argumentative theory:[12]

> The main problem posed by communication in an evolutionary context is that of deceiving interlocutors. When I am talking to you, if you accept everything I say, then it's going to be fairly easy for me to manipulate you into doing things that you shouldn't be doing. And as a result, people have a whole suite of mechanisms that are called epistemic vigilance, which they use to evaluate what other people tell them.
>
> If you tell me something that disagrees with what I already believe, my first reaction is going to be to reject what you're telling me, because otherwise I could be vulnerable. But then you have a problem. If you tell me something that I disagree with, and I just reject your opinion, then maybe actually you were right and maybe I was wrong, and you have to find a way to convince me. This is where reasoning kicks in. You have an incentive to convince me, so you're going to start using reasons, and I'm going to have to evaluate these reasons. That's why we think reasoning evolved.

That we reason, however, is not enough. It's *how* we reason that makes the most difference as to how successful that reasoning is in getting us the right answer. When we reason alone, it works poorly. When we reason in groups of people who disagree, we reason better.

> [L]et's say you have a quarrel with your partner, and you go to brood over what happened in your room. And you keep thinking about why it was all his or her fault, and why you did everything that was possible to make things right, and you know it really has nothing to do with you. You find many, many reasons why you didn't do anything wrong, and it's all the other person's fault.
>
> On the other hand, if you had discussed the same thing with someone who might have been more neutral, then that person might

---

[12] Hugo Mercier, "The Argumentative Theory," interview by John Brockman, *Edge*, April 27, 2011, http://edge.org/conversation/the-argumentative-theory.

have been able to tell you that perhaps you did something that wasn't quite right, and maybe there your partner was actually correct. In our lives, it is important to keep in mind the pitfalls that individual reasoning can lead us to, and this can stop us from making poor decisions because we've been trapped by our confirmation bias.

When we surround ourselves with media that continually agrees with our viewpoint, we are essentially reasoning with those who already agree with us. This stunts our reasoning and dooms us to inaccurate conclusions and poorer opinions. It is entirely natural—perhaps imperative—for us to resist opposing viewpoints, but *resisting* is not the same as *ignoring*. It is a good idea to make those who hold differing views work to reason with us, but if we shut down any possibility to be convinced otherwise, we're wasting everyone's time and are dooming ourselves to an echo chamber where no new information can penetrate.

Choosing the Right Sources

"Faced with the choice between changing one's mind and proving that there is no need to do so, almost everyone gets busy on the proof." – John Kenneth Galbraith

It's very important that we choose our information sources carefully. There are two types of sources in the world: primary and secondary. Primary sources are the actual source of the information. Secondary sources are anything relaying that information afterwards.

If you read an article about a new scientific discovery, the article is a secondary source. The primary source is the peer-reviewed, published study that the article is referencing. If you hear a friend tell you about what Sam said, your friend is the secondary source and Sam is the primary. It's OK to start with secondary sources, but when you're challenging your beliefs, it's really important to find the primary sources instead. You may be surprised how often secondary sources, inadvertently or purposefully, take primary sources out of context to satisfy their own agendas. If you are forced to choose a secondary source, I have some suggestions for standards to hold them to:

1. Do they correct themselves and admit when they are wrong? News is fast-paced, and sometimes people jump the gun. Do they go out of their way to make sure that their audience knows they were wrong when they discover it?

2. Do they allow and encourage opposing viewpoints? Opposing viewpoints encourage critical thought in the speakers and listeners, or the writers and readers. For some, it will be the first exposure to any opposing viewpoint.

3. Do they explain their reasoning? If they preach about their beliefs without explaining their thought processes, this is a red flag. Someone who shares their conclusions without their thought process to arrive at them is depriving you of knowing what is behind those conclusions. Be wary of those who are unable to tell you about the journey to their conclusion. They may be peddling a belief they don't actually hold or one they have blindly accepted from someone else.

4. Do they link to their source(s) and encourage their readers to form their own judgments? These sources should be primary sources, not other secondary sources. Meaning they should be the actual artifact being opined about or the actual person involved or someone who was present. Quoting other secondary sources doesn't count, nor does prefacing opinions with "some people say" or "critics say."

5. Do they avoid financial conflicts of interest? Money is powerful, and it's permeating our media in unprecedented and insidious ways. Some journalists are even posting articles under their bylines but are being paid to write them by corporate or political interests. Remember to follow the money whenever you want to understand motives.

Your mind is the result of what goes into it. It's important to feed your mind a balanced diet of opposing views and be open to challenging long-held beliefs if they don't stand up to the evidence or the reality of your life.

What information have you been consuming up to now about homosexuality? Where did it come from? Does it stand up to the truth of your experience? Is it coming from a place of fear and hate, or a place of love? Are you exposing yourself to opposing ideas? Are you confusing someone's opinions with facts? As we learned in Chapter 1: Your Mind. Friend or Foe?, our minds reach (and blaze through) a juncture where we decide to use actual data vs. judged data when forming our reality about any given topic. We should not underestimate the ways in which the media we consume contributes to our judged data about it.

Chapter 6: Gay Rights

"It takes no compromise to give people their rights . . . it takes no money to respect the individual. It takes no political deal to give people freedom. It takes no survey to remove repression."

— Harvey Milk

By the evening of June 28, 1969, tensions were reaching new levels. At just after 1 a.m., the police raided the Stone Wall Inn, a gay bar in New York's Greenwich Village neighborhood. The raid was not going the way previous raids had gone. Some of the participants were sent through the front door and told to leave, but instead of complying, they stood outside. A crowd soon formed as residents of the mostly gay neighborhood began coming out to see what was going on. They joined the recently ejected bar patrons, and the anger became palpable. Word began spreading through the crowd that patrons inside the bar were being assaulted and lesbians were being touched inappropriately during frisking.

When the patrol wagons finally appeared to begin taking those who were being arrested to jail, some of the police began roughing up the handcuffed patrons on the way out to the wagons. One lesbian, who had a laceration on her head from being hit with a police baton, fell as police were trying to throw her into the wagon. As she fell down, she looked up at the crowd and yelled, "Why don't you guys do something?" An officer threw her into the wagon, and at that moment the crowd became an angry mob. The fighting lasted off and on for days with injuries on both sides. One thing was certain; the days of gays passively taking abuse from the police were over. To this day, gay rights parades worldwide celebrate the Stonewall riots throughout the month of June as the beginning of the fight for equality in America. Although gay recorded history goes back centuries, the modern political struggle for gay rights in the United States can mostly be traced back to this single event in New York on June 28, 1969.

The journey to Stonewall was not a friendly one. In the decade that followed World War II, gays faced immeasurable discrimination from society at large. Psychology, a relatively new field of science, was anxious to prove itself and allowed what should have been a nonbiased look at homosexuality to be influenced by the social stigma of the era. It's as if psychologists set out to prove there was something wrong with gays rather than challenging the notion of gender norms in the 1950s.

If women were "the lesser sex" as many men believed—and unfortunately often still do—then gay men represented a serious challenge to masculinity itself. Because of this now debunked "science," there were many laws on the books against gays in the decade or so leading up to Stonewall. Raids on gay bars (usually owned by the mafia) were common. Women who were wearing less than three items of feminine clothing were arrested; men wearing feminine clothing were also taken in. Everyone was required to show ID, and if the sex didn't match the look of the person, they were arrested. Transvestites were taken into the back room by police officers and their sexes were confirmed. It was these very raids that eventually led to the riots described above.

To be clear, the fight for gay rights is better described as "equal rights for gay people." Gay people are not asking for "special" rights. Just the same rights and protections that heterosexual people and other minorities enjoy. In the sections below, we'll explore two of the areas that affect gay people's rights in daily life.

Serving in the Military

Technical Sergeant Leonard Matlovich was the first gay service member to purposely out himself in 1975 to fight the military's ban on gays. After he died of complications from AIDS, he was buried in the Congressional Cemetery. His tombstone reads: "A Gay Vietnam Veteran: When I was in the military, they gave me a medal for killing two men and a discharge for loving one."

Prior to 1994, the US military discharged soldiers who engaged in or admitted engaging in homosexual activity. In 1994, President Bill Clinton signed a compromise with military leadership that came to be known as "Don't Ask, Don't Tell" (DADT). The intention of the compromise was that gay men and women could join the military and any questions about orientation would be stricken from the application process. As long as those men and women didn't openly discuss their homosexuality, they would be allowed to serve.

In reality, however, keeping sexual orientation secret in such a close-knit environment turned out to be nearly impossible, and once it was discovered or confessed, dishonorable discharges were often the result. This was the same action taken against numerous military service members before DADT, so the law had the twisted effect of allowing gay people to sign up for service only to be likely discharged in the same fashion as before the law.

The repeal of DADT and full acceptance of homosexuals into military service didn't occur until several years into President Obama's first term in 2010, with the official end date for the policy of September 20, 2011. In 2017, President Trump issued a policy change via tweet that prohibits transgendered soldiers from serving in the military. The White House provided no details about what would happen to the estimated nearly ten thousand transgendered troops in active and reserve duty. As I write this, the matter is still being challenged in court with the Trump administration requesting that the, now-conservative majority Supreme Court, fast-track the case.

Same-Sex Marriage

Clay Greene and Harold Scull lived in California. Clay was eighty-eight years old and Harold was seventy-seven. They'd been partners for twenty years. In 2008, Scull was admitted to the hospital with a black eye. Initially Scull reported that he was the victim of abuse from Greene, but then he recanted and refused to file a formal complaint. After Scull fell seriously ill shortly afterwards, Greene alleged in a lawsuit that as his partner lay dying in a hospital bed, officials denied visitation rights and ignored signed wills, medical declarations, and powers of attorney, naming each as the other's spouse. The suit claimed that officials forced Greene into a nursing home and then sold off the couple's household belongings, including art and other heirlooms, carting off choice pieces for themselves. Greene was never allowed to see his partner before he passed away. According to the county's attorney, Gregory Spaulding:

> "The dispute might have been avoided if the men had been able to be legally married or if they had registered as domestic partners.

Because they weren't, their funds were viewed as separate. Marital status played a role in what options were available to them."[13]

Sometimes it's the family of one of the partners that denies the other partner. Shane Bitney Crone and Tom Bridegroom were in a loving, committed relationship. In 2011, Bridegroom died when he fell off a rooftop while taking photos of a friend. Crone was not allowed to attend his partner's funeral. The story was made into a documentary called *Bridegroom.*

> "I received a phone call from one of Tom's relatives, and she wanted to let me know that I wasn't welcome to attend his funeral," Crone says. "Because if I do show up, his uncle and his father had planned an attack."[14]

Imagine if your husband or wife's family could prevent you from seeing your spouse while they lay in the hospital after a car accident or could prevent you from attending their funeral? These are just two examples out of thousands of gay couples who were denied basic rights and dignity merely because they were not married.

In the 2000s, it seemed everyone on the left wanted to support marriage equality, but very few seemed to have the political will to step up and begin truly advocating for it. It wasn't until President Obama voiced support for full marriage rights for gays in 2012, a position he was rumored to hold personally for years before he was president, that the tide began to change with several prominent Democrats and even a few Republicans jumping on board shortly after.

Even so, it wasn't until 2015 that the Supreme Court ruling in the case Obergefell v. Hodges forced all fifty states to legalize gay marriage. This ruling effectively overturned the Defense of Marriage Act.

---

[13] Paul Payne, "Guerneville Man Settles Suit against Sonoma County for $600,000," *The Press Democrat,* July 22, 2010, http://www.pressdemocrat.com/news/2237322-181/guerneville-man-settles-suit-against?page=0.

[14] Lynn Okura, "'Bridegroom,' Heartbreaking Documentary about Unmarried Gay Couple, to Premiere on OWN," *Huffington Post,* updated October 7, 2013, www.huffingtonpost.com/2013/10/07/bridegroom-documentary-own_n_4046247.html.

That's the history, but you may not be convinced that gays should be allowed to get married. If that describes you, it's my aim to give you some food for thought on the topic.

To begin with, let's agree that marriage is a legal contract. At its core, it is a legally recognized relationship that bestows both participants with rights and protections. If you don't believe that, ask yourself the following question: When we want to end a marriage, who do we call? A priest or a lawyer?

While many of us associate marriage (a legal construct) with weddings (a ceremony), in fact it is perfectly possible to have that contract without a full-fledged, white-flowers-in-the-garden wedding—or even a religious officiant. One can get married by any justice of the peace, cruise ship captain, county clerk, or Elvis impersonator—and many couples do.

I bring this up not to be flippant or disrespectful to those more beautiful ceremonies. By the time you read this, I'll have had one of those ceremonies myself, getting married to my partner of fifteen years. Instead, I'm pointing out that the right to enter into a marriage contract is what gays have been fighting for. It isn't—and has never been—to force any church of any denomination to perform the wedding *ceremony*.

What we *do* want is to have our relationships treated with respect in the eyes of the law. We want the responsibilities that come with it—to be there for the other in sickness and in health. We want the stability that marriage provides to heterosexual couples through inheritance, child custody, immigration, social security, and many other legal protections. Not to mention, we'd like the law to be on our side if someone decides we aren't to be allowed to see our sick or dying partner.

In fact, if you are a fiscal conservative, gay marriage is a win from these standpoints as well. As the gay author and blogger Andrew Sullivan argued in his landmark article for the New Republic way back in 1989 entitled "Here Comes the Groom: A (Conservative) Case for Gay Marriage":[15]

---

[15]Andrew Sullivan, "Here Comes the Groom: A (Conservative) Case for Gay Marriage," *New Republic*, August 27, 1989, http://www.newrepublic.com/article/79054/here-comes-the-groom.

Society has good reason to extend legal advantages to heterosexuals who choose the formal sanction of marriage over simply living together. They make a deeper commitment to one another and to society; in exchange, society extends certain benefits to them. Marriage provides an anchor, if an arbitrary and weak one, in the chaos of sex and relationships to which we are all prone. It provides a mechanism for emotional stability, economic security, and the healthy rearing of the next generation.

Sullivan correctly points out that when one spouse in a marriage falls ill or loses a job, it is the other spouse who helps support this person before they fall to social programs that cost taxpayers money. Unmarried people often have no choice but to rely on these programs immediately. Fiscal conservatives would likely encourage the legal bond that marriage offers so that government spending and size can be kept low.

Defeated opponents of same-sex marriage have now taken to saying that allowing two people of the same gender to enter a legal agreement for marriage somehow violates the former's religious freedom. Which religion (Christianity) seems to be assumed. It seems ironic that the First Amendment, which is intended to protect *all* religions, is being used by *one* of them to limit the rights of everyone else.

Today, there are elected government officials who claim that their individual religious rights take precedence over their legal obligations to issue marriage licenses in accordance with the law. I wonder, would they use the same argument if a Muslim Department of Motor Vehicles employee refused to issue a driver's license to a woman?

There is one more aspect of the same-sex marriage topic that I'd like to tackle before we move on, and that is the notion of "traditional marriage." Most critics of same-sex marriage claim that it is a violation of "traditional marriage" and that we must fight to protect it (now we'll see why the name of the law "The Defense of Marriage Act" is so ironic).

Traditional Marriage

If you ask a historian about traditional marriage, they'll usually shrug and ask, "Which century? Where on the planet?"

According to the Bible, King Solomon had seven hundred wives and three hundred concubines. Polygamy was common in China, Africa, and with American Mormons in the nineteenth century. When you consider that the first evidence of marriage contracts and ceremonies dates to four thousand years ago, it's a relatively recent development to consider marriage as a sexually exclusive, romantic union between one man and one woman. Two centuries ago, that kind of marriage was very rare.

If the definition of "traditional" infers historical, we have thousands of years of polygamy and women being treated as property to hold up against the last two centuries of relative gender equality in marriage. Clearly today's monogamous (even straight) version of marriage is what broke the "traditional" marriage model.

Even allowing gays to marry isn't a new development. Up until the thirteenth century, male-bonding ceremonies called "spiritual brotherhoods" were common in churches across the Mediterranean. They included the recital of marriage prayers, the joining of hands at the altar, and a ceremonial kiss. It wasn't until 1306 that Byzantine Emperor Andronicus II declared these ceremonies, along with sorcery and incest, to be unchristian.[16]

In my travels to Europe, I've been reminded how young America is. The world's civilizations have existed long before America was formed. It's easy for Americans to fall into the trap of believing that our country's history is on the same scale as world history, but this is a huge flaw in our thinking, and it colors our use of the word "traditional" in the case of marriage and other topics. This same flaw prevents us from noticing how much civilization existed before and after Jesus lived and how different those cultures were during the eras represented by the Bible. It's with (I hope) this expanded perspective that we will explore religion and homosexuality in the next chapter.

---

[16] "How Marriage Has Changed over Centuries," *The Week*, June 1, 2012, http://theweek.com/articles/475141/how-marriage-changed-over-centuries.

Chapter 7: Homosexuality and Religion

"In general, Christians have not been very good about loving gay people. Oh, they'll tell you they hate the sin but they love the sinner, but I don't see much love for the sinner."

— Ed Dobson, former VP of Moral Majority, Inc.

"Anyone who does not provide for their relatives, and especially for their own household, has denied the faith and is worse than an unbeliever."

— 1 Timothy 5:8

"It's a survival thing. In America, we lose six queer kids a day to the street. That is, every four hours a queer kid dies, whether it be from freezing to death or getting the shit beat out of them or a drug overdose. This is our next real plague."

— Rick Westbrook

Who This Chapter Is For

In the first part of this chapter, I want to introduce you to a few real gay teenagers who have lived or do live in religious households. It's my hope that you'll see the lack of humanity in what so many of these kids are going through.

In the remainder of the chapter, we will take a brief look at the various passages in the Bible that are often cited against gays. This is not intended to be a full treatment of the topic, however. There are great authors who have more religious credibility than I do who have written about religion and homosexuality. Please see Appendix B: Recommended Resources for a list of books and articles from these folks.

Though we will primarily be discussing Christianity, we will briefly touch upon Islam as well as there are some parallels specifically surrounding LGBT acceptance.

My Confession

I have a confession: I'm not a religious person. Despite the lack of church attendance in my upbringing, I do believe in God; it's just that, for me, I couldn't buy into the God that religion wanted me to see. That God is described as less capable of unconditional love than my dog, and that couldn't be right. The Old Testament describes a rather insecure God who punishes those who don't worship Him and do as He commands. I wondered how God could be so powerful but be unable to conquer pride, ego, jealousy, and anger—the very things humans fall victim to.

This left me with a spiritual gap that went unfilled during my young adult years. I found myself confounded by the beauty and complexity of the universe—and the question that still boggles scientific minds: What caused the Big Bang? What was there before that? While most scientists study the laws of physics and astrophysics, I wanted to understand *how they came to be*. For me, that always pointed to God—a position I find completely compatible with science but incompatible with religion.

In my early thirties, a mentor handed me a copy of *Conversations with God* by Neale Donald Walsch. I found that I couldn't put it down. This was more like the God I knew in my heart. Rather than Eastern vs. Western philosophy, it was Eastern *meets* Western philosophy. It connected science and religion. It painted a picture of a God that loved *everyone* universally and equally—gay, straight, skinny, fat, warts and all.

So, it's with this lens on religion and God that I view with sadness and disappointment the way that some parents use what they believe to be the word of God against children at a time when those children are deeply confused about the differences they're sensing compared to the rest of their friends. You'll read a few examples of that below.

Real Stories, Real Teenagers

There's a scene from the 1989 movie *Parenthood* where Steve Martin's character, Gil, is having a discussion with his father, Frank (played by Jason Robards), about Gil's brother Larry (played by Tom Hulce). Larry is a bit of a mess. He's constantly swindling the family out of money and going after the next get-rich-quick scheme while shirking responsibilities including taking care of a child out of wedlock. In the scene, Frank is asking his son (Larry's brother) Gil for advice because if he doesn't come up with thousands of dollars, the mob is going to kill Larry. The scene goes like this:

> **Gil:** "You got that kind of money?"
> **Frank:** "I got it but . . . it's gonna hurt. I wanted to retire next year, and this will put that off for a while. A long while. I never should have had four! You know when you were two years old, we thought you had polio. You know about that?"
> **Gil:** "Yeah, Mom once said something . . ."
> **Frank:** "Yeah, well, for a week we didn't know. I hated you for that."
> **Gil:** "What?"
> **Frank:** "I did. I—I hated having to go through that. The caring, the worrying, the pain. That's not for me. And you know it's not like that all ends when you're eighteen or twenty-one or forty-one or sixty-one. It never, never ends! It's like your Aunt Edna's ass. It goes on forever and is just as frightening."

Gil: (laughs) "That's true."

Frank: "There is no end zone. You never cross the goal line, spike the ball, and do your touchdown dance. Never. I'm sixty-four and Larry is twenty-seven, and he's still my son. Like Kevin is your son. You think I want him to get hurt? He's my son."

For most parents, disowning a child or putting them in a situation where they can be hurt seems unthinkable—even when they behave in ways the parent doesn't agree with. Yet it happens repeatedly with gay youth—especially those who live in deeply religious households. LGBT people make up roughly 5 percent of the youth population overall, but they make up an estimated 40 percent of the homeless youth population. The Center for American Progress has reported that there are between 320,000 and 400,000 homeless LGBT youths in the United States. One study estimates that up to 40 percent of LGBT homeless youth leave home due to family rejection.[17] The numbers are staggering. That so many of these homeless teens come from homes that work so diligently to protect the lives of the unborn further confounds me, for how can someone claim to be pro-life and yet willfully endanger the life of their own offspring?

For gays who are religious or who were brought up in religious families, being openly gay can mean not only facing the judgment of their friends, their family, and their extended social circle (which is also often religious), but also facing a fear of judgment from a God they were brought up to believe doesn't love them.

The amount of judgment and ostracizing that gays suffer at the hands of religion is often more than they can handle. A 2009 study, "Family Rejection as a Predictor of Negative Health Outcomes," led by Dr. Caitlin Ryan and published in the journal *Pediatrics*[18] concluded that lesbian, gay, and bisexual young

---

[17] Alex Morris, "The Forsaken: A Rising Number of Homeless Gay Teens Are Being Cast Out by Religious Families," *Rolling Stone*, September 3, 2014, www.rollingstone.com/culture/features/the-forsaken-a-rising-number-of-homeless-gay-teens-are-being-cast-out-by-religious-families-20140903.

[18] Caitlin Ryan, et al., "Family Rejection as a Predictor of Negative Health Outcomes in White and Latino Lesbian, Gay, and Bisexual Young Adults," *Pediatrics* 123, no. 1 (January 2009), https://pediatrics.aappublications.org/content/123/1/346.

adults who reported higher levels of family rejection during adolescence were 8.4 times more likely to report having attempted suicide. It's a sad reality that so many gays in religious homes are only allowed to be a part of their families, churches, and social circles if they hide who they really are.

Have you struggled with what it means to love your kid unconditionally while holding strong to your beliefs? Perhaps you have considered removing your support and shelter as some kind of leverage. If so, please consider the true stories below. (Names and some minor details have been changed to protect the identities of those who shared their stories with me.)

Ricardo

Ricardo is a gay seventeen-year-old young man who lives with his family in a Hispanic community. His entire family is Catholic, and while he believes religion plays a role in his family's homophobia, it's not the entire picture. He says, "My entire life, I've lived in places where being LGBT is something shameful. Latino society is plagued with male chauvinism and homophobia. Everyone makes fun of gay people and tries to avoid them."

Ricardo believes that his mother, the most religious member of the family, thinks of gay people as mistakes. When she started to suspect that he was gay, she gave him an ultimatum: "If you're going to be like that, then when you're eighteen I'm not going to have anything else to do with you. You get out of high school and that's it. You're on your own."

Ricardo doesn't understand the rejection. He tells me, "How can the people who are supposed to love you, care about you, and look after you unconditionally be so quick to pass judgment and turn their backs against you just because you're a little different from the norm? I mean, I'm still me. The same Ricardo whose diapers they changed when he was a baby. The same Ricardo that gets good grades and always does his chores. And the same Ricardo that has always liked boys—the only thing that's changed is that now you know about it."

When I asked him what would happen if he came out, he replied, "I'd get kicked out of the house and would get no financial support from my family. I'd essentially be homeless and broke." He adds, "I hate being with my family. They will never understand me. They will never let me be me. They value *their* reputations and beliefs over *my* happiness, over their child. Someday I'll have to choose between them and me, and I will choose me every time. I know I'll go to my wedding alone. I know I won't see them anymore after college. I'll write to them, I'll try to call, but I know *for sure* they won't answer."

Ryan

Ryan is a fifteen-year-old bisexual male. His family is deeply religious, and he says that being anything but straight with religious parents is "a really unpredictable experience. Even the most mature and educated parents could react badly." Because he holds this belief, he's decided not to come out to anybody in his family until he is completely independent—which he defines as "out of college, stable job, maybe a boyfriend."

He says that his parents and members of his extended family hold the belief that being gay is a result of a traumatic experience during childhood. He says that they believe if a gay person repents their "gay sins," they will become straight and that a person cannot be born gay.

While this sounds like an intellectual challenge for Ryan, the fact is that the stakes are high. "If I were to come out as bisexual to my parents at this current time, I would most likely be kicked out or sent somewhere. I've never brought up the subject of me being bisexual to my parents, so I'm obviously not sure of this, but judging from the attitude of all my family members, this is extremely likely."

Ryan says that much of his parents' negative reactions will likely be caused by embarrassment. "My extended family believes that being gay stems from childhood trauma, so if I came out, they would blame my parents." When I asked him how he felt about the impending disconnection with his family, he expressed sadness. "I have a great relationship with my grandparents, and I wish that my kids could have that."

Ironically, the fact that Ryan's parents and family will cut ties with him for religious reasons has driven him to change his views about God. "I do believe there is a god, but that He is not as judgmental and hateful as the people in my church."

Daryl

Daryl's story was one of the hardest ones for me to write. The reason for that will become clear soon. He wouldn't tell me his story until I promised not to involve anyone to help him and promised not to pity him. These were very difficult promises for me to make. I tell his story here in the hopes that religious parents might learn how badly this can go if they blame their gay child for their own discomfort and fear.

Daryl is a seventeen-year-old gay teen who came out to his friends when he was a freshman in high school. His father was a pastor, as were all the males in his family. One day, his parents saw a post on Facebook that revealed he was gay. His parents confronted him and asked if he was gay. When he said yes, they did not react well. "My dad was just staring off into the distance, and my mom began to cry. It was all too much for me, so I went into my room. My brother came inside a few minutes later and handed me a Bible, saying, 'Do you really think of yourself as so ugly that you're just going to date guys?'"

The next few months were the toughest in his life. His parents sent him to counseling, but he quickly figured out that the counselor was more interested in convincing him that he wasn't really gay than helping him or helping his parents come to terms with the truth. His parents then informed him that he would be homeschooled. Without a cell phone or a laptop, he would be cut off from all of his friends instantly. "I was crushed. I ate so much that day." Daryl had been stress-eating since he came out and had gained almost twenty pounds in just few months.

In the meantime, his father lost his job as a pastor. The church where he was the treasurer was short on money, and the head pastor blamed him. His father had been abusive to Daryl his whole life—verbally and sometimes physically—so this development didn't improve the situation. His dad, desperate for work, moved back to his home country of Argentina and took Daryl with him. The decision was so sudden that Daryl isn't even sure if it was by force. He was placed in a Christian homeschool there. The only place he could interact with people was church. Desperate, he began to search for companionship online. He found a twenty-year-old. At fifteen, with no guidance, no one to turn to for advice, he made the mistake of having unprotected sex with him.

Daryl began to suffer the consequences of isolation. He started to cut his wrists and was suffering from depression. He eventually tried his own aversion therapy to try to "cure" his homosexuality. He says, "I began to masturbate to lesbian pornography to avoid seeing naked males. Then I would watch gay porn, and when I got an erection, I would stab myself with a pen or a knife."

He began to fantasize that he was someone else. When he was home alone, he would pretend to be a famous singer singing at the top of his lungs. "It got to the point where I couldn't tell what was real and what wasn't. I had a huge fear that I would wake up one day in a hospital because I was crazy. The nights were the worst because that was when I could reflect on what I really was. I would cry every night. I couldn't breathe. I didn't want to be alone. I was so scared. I thought I was alone and no one wanted me. I hadn't talked to anyone in over two years, and I wanted to die. I got a belt every night and hung it over my door, putting it around my neck hoping I could slide farther and farther down to just die." His relationship with his father continued to deteriorate. "My dad and I got into a fight one day. He hit me and I fell to the ground. I got up and ran to the laundry room outside scared because I didn't know who to talk to or where to go."

That's about when the symptoms started. "I was showing signs of HIV. I realized then that this was finally a way to die. It would be slow, but at least I could stop trying to figure out how to kill myself. I don't want treatment for it because I don't want to live." His parents divorced and he moved back in with his mother. When he got back to the United States, he had a fear of people. He says, "I was breathless being surrounded by so many kids." Daryl began to isolate himself again. To escape the loneliness at night, he would binge-watch television and eventually began to watch the Harry Potter movies. As an escape, he now reads nonstop and wants to write his own books so that "one day, someone might read my books just to escape their life the way I escaped mine."

As I finish typing this paragraph, I have tears of sadness and frustration streaming down my face. I promised Daryl no pity and I kept my word to him, but I have a pointed question that is seared into my mind: How far have Christians strayed from Christ's teachings when they think that He would approve of this treatment of another human being in His name?

Alex

Not all experiences with religion and homosexuality are negative, of course, and stories like Alex's brought me hope that there is a way for a religious community to come together in a supportive, loving way for LGBT kids. Alex figured out that he was gay at fourteen but kept it to himself. At fifteen, he started dating a boy. After his mom inadvertently walked in on him making out with his boyfriend, it was time to come out. When he told his parents he was gay, they just shrugged and said they were both happy for him and they just wanted to see him happy.

Alex is now twenty and is very involved with his church as a teacher. Over the past several years, he's had to come out several times to various church leaders who have all embraced him and supported him. He decided it was time to tell the kids he teaches. He typed the following message to them via a group message: "Hey guys, I haven't been completely honest with all of you. I expect honesty from you guys and received tons of it last year. I tried to say this earlier but chickened out, so I'm saying it now. I'm gay. I hope this doesn't change anything with us and that we have a great second year together." Within fifteen minutes, they had all replied both publicly and privately with total support. "I was so overwhelmed that I started crying my eyes out because I was so overjoyed."

I asked him what he thought made the difference between his church, which has been so accepting of him, and others that are so much less accepting of LGBT people. He said, "I think the difference is that some churches understand what it means to love one another. They also realize that the world is changing and adapting to society is important. But there are some Catholic churches that say moving with the times is idiotic and that 'the church will move the world, not the other way around,' but the only way the church will move the world is by loving everything and accepting everybody."

You Can't Punish the Gay Away

Stories like Ricardo's, Ryan's, and Daryl's are far from rare. Religious parents placing minor children in "pray the gay away" camps that amount to sanctioned prison camps often in foreign countries are not rare enough. I've personally helped a teen who was posting messages from the streets his parents had kicked him to for being gay. He had been living there for several days and was getting cold and hungry. He was starting to consider prostitution to make survival money because the hunger was getting so painful. Others got him to a shelter for gay youth through online posting. To this day, I don't know if he's OK, or even what his real name was. I can only hope that he found a safe place to live and warm food to eat.

I can't even begin to describe for you the feeling I get in the pit of my stomach when I interact with these kids. Their fear and loneliness are palpable. Everything they knew about life was just taken away for simply being who they were born to be. Otherwise supportive, loving parents often just walk away and don't look back.

The only way I've been able to understand how a parent can do this is to think that they're hoping to convince their kid how seriously they disapprove of their homosexuality. It's as if they're thinking, "I'll show him. If he insists on being gay, he can see what it's like in the real world. I'm sure he'll come around to my way of seeing things before long." This is a heavily flawed and dangerous way of thinking. You will not punish the gay out of your child. Instead, you are placing him or her in a very dangerous, potentially fatal situation over something they have as much control over as they do their eye color.

As a parent, you have only two choices: Love your child for who they really are or love them conditionally for who you want them to be (or not to be). If you choose conditional love and think you are being true to God by doing so, then perhaps you believe God's love for you is conditional too. If you belong to a Christian-based religion, here is some Biblical evidence to counter that thought. (For the purposes of this discussion, I'll be mostly using the New International Version of the Bible unless otherwise noted.)

> "Whoever does not love, does not know God, because God is love." – 1 John 4:8

> "If I speak in the tongues of men and of angels, but do not have love, I am only a resounding gong or a clanging cymbal. If I have the gift of prophesy and can fathom all mysteries and all knowledge, and if I have a faith that can move mountains, but do not have love, I am nothing. If I give all I possess to the poor and give over my body to hardship that I may boast, but do not have love, I gain nothing.
> "Love is patient, love is kind. It does not envy, it does not boast, it is not proud. It does not dishonor others, it is not self-seeking, it is not easily angered, it keeps no record of wrongs. Love does not delight in evil but rejoices with the truth. It always protects, always trusts, always hopes, always perseveres." – 1 Corinthians 13:1-7

> "But I am like an olive tree flourishing in the house of God; I trust in God's unfailing love for ever and ever." – Psalm 52:8b

Your son or daughter's homosexuality is not going to disappear because you threaten to put them on the street. Nor is that showing love—the tough kind or otherwise. At most, all that will happen is they will suppress their truth from you so *you* will be more comfortable.

Shame vs. Religion

If you're having a negative, punitive reaction to homosexuality and believe your religion justifies this, is it possible that you may be embarrassed by your child's sexuality and are lashing out because of it? It isn't difficult to imagine that Daryl's parents are reacting out of shame for *themselves.* His father and many of the males in his family are pastors. Perhaps it isn't their religion that causes his parents to react so terribly. Perhaps it's a shame about homosexuality that is borne in the church they attend and the people they attend it with.

Ryan's family believes that being a homosexual is a defect caused by childhood trauma. This false belief creates a sense of blame and shame that surrounds those in his life because if there was childhood trauma, they would likely be accused of being responsible for it. His parents are so eager to protect their own reputations that they will do anything to convince him he's really not gay and, when it becomes undeniable, they will likely wipe him from their lives like something that never existed.

There is another choice. Remove the shame from homosexuality to begin with. Make the shameful act the one about abandoning children. Might this be *your* challenge, not theirs? Your challenge from God to demonstrate the same unconditional love toward your child that you receive from Him? When church leaders perpetuate shame about homosexuality, they are doing a disservice to the truth, to their members, and to gay people and their families.

Interpreting Religious Texts

Note: If religion doesn't play a role in your issues surrounding homosexuality, you can safely skip the rest of this chapter unless you are just curious about the topic.

The more I learn about history, the more I realize that human beings are flawed. We make mistakes. We are too sure of ourselves when we should be humble and too humble when we should be sure of ourselves. We are highly manipulable through emotions. When we are scared, we make heroes out of charlatans and enemies out of people who are different than us in some way that these "leaders" tell us is supposed to be important, whether it be skin color, heritage, birthplace, sexual orientation, or gender. Religion isn't immune to these human flaws. In fact, because they deal with human morality, religions can actually make these flaws more pronounced. The fact that religious texts are curated by human beings over millennia and religions are practiced by human beings means that unavoidable human flaws are introduced along the way.

If you ask the question, "Is [insert my religion] against homosexuality?" I would tell you that it depends on your zip code, the era you are alive in, the particular church you attend, the particular religious leader your church has hired, the particular version of the religious text they are reading from, and that particular leader's *interpretation* of that text on that day. That's a whole lot of human being between you and the word of God.

Language is a double-edged sword for humans. On one hand, it allows us to pass knowledge down through generations and to evolve faster as a species. On the other hand, it's quite imprecise and open to misunderstanding. If I say, "You look nice today!" you might respond back with, "What do you mean 'today'?"—and that doesn't even involve a translation from one language to another! The translation from language to language introduces much more complexity. As Helen Glanville and Murtha Baca wrote in their essay entitled "Issues and Challenges in Translating Historical Texts" [emphasis added]:

> Translation always represents a shift not only between two languages but also between two cultures. A translator must take into account factors that are linguistic or semantic as well as, broadly speaking, cultural. *Every translation is, to a greater or lesser extent, also an interpretation.*
>
> Translations, as much as the original work in question, rely on a common field of reference between the writer and the reader. This obviously becomes more difficult as we cross not only geographical

and linguistic frontiers but also temporal ones; *the past is indeed a foreign country.*[19]

This makes sense. Culturally speaking, the United States in 1800 is much different than the one in the 2000s. What we find morally and socially acceptable today is entirely different from then. Christianity and Islam have been around for two thousand and fourteen hundred years respectively. If you were directly related to someone who lived during Jesus Christ's time, and each generation lived an average of fifty years, your relative would be something like your great-great-[insert thirty-eight more "greats"]-grandparent. Most of us have had the experience where an elder relative said something cringeworthy at the dinner table, and we usually have no problem dismissing them and their comment as outdated. Why can't we at least acknowledge that forty earlier generations of ancestors, each with different cultures and political structures, influenced the Bible with each translation?

Imagine the cultural, linguistic, and semantic differences at play, not to mention the power of literally wielding the word of a god at the tip of your pen. Popes, imams, kings, and political rulers of the past surely influenced these translations, if not directly, then indirectly through enforcement of cultural norms for their time period. When a priest, pastor, imam, minister, or rabbi stands before their flock and reads from their book and then applies that to current life, they are making an interpretation of that text.

Even if we accept that the Bible, in its original Hebrew, Aramaic, and Greek, was the word of God (and I'm not arguing here either way), we must acknowledge that it's likely that our modern Bibles represent many hops in a game of telephone played by human beings. In fact, Islam specifically says that if a Qur'an has been translated from its original Arabic (or doesn't at

---

[19] Helen Glanville and Murtha Baca, "Issues and Challenges in Translating Historical Texts" in Murtha Baca et al., *Pietro Mellini's Inventory in Verse, 1681: A Digital Facsimile with Translation and Commentary* (Los Angeles: Getty Research Institute, 2014), http://hdl.handle.net/10020/mellini/e9.

least contain it), it is, by definition, an interpretation and not a real Qur'an. We'll see how this language problem affects the topic of homosexuality shortly when we study some of the most common Biblical verses used against it.

A Word About Islam

Just studying Islam's historical grappling with homosexuality can make one dizzy. Whether practitioners of Islam accept homosexuality, tolerate it, or behead you for it depends on whether you get in an airplane or a time machine. Historically, the entire spectrum of tolerance depends upon factors that change so often and across such a wide variety of Muslim countries and cultures that you should look it up online to see the latest information. This is especially true if you're gay and travelling to a primarily Muslim country outside of the United States.

In traditional Islam, there seemed to be general agreement that penetrative homosexual intercourse was the same as unlawful heterosexual intercourse. Where there was wide disagreement was what the appropriate punishment should have been for it. It could have resulted in anything from nothing at all, to flogging, to capital punishment. Even contemporary scholars disagree on these matters. American Islam scholar Kecia Ali notes that "there is no one Muslim perspective on anything,"[20] and that presents a problem for Muslim LGBT people. At this point in time, you can ask ten different Muslims and get eight different answers on the topic.

If the stakes weren't so high, I'd be suggesting a shrug and a "don't ask, don't tell" approach here. Unfortunately, depending on where you live, some of you may face massive repercussions for revealing your sexual orientation while practicing Islam, so you should use caution before doing so.

---

[20] Kecia Ali, *Sexual Ethics and Islam: Feminist Reflections on Qur'an, Hadith, and Jurisprudence* (London: Oneworld Publications, 2016), xvi, 103.

At first glance, the situation doesn't look good. It's fairly disheartening how widespread the nonacceptance of homosexuality is among Muslim nations. A 2013 Pew Research Center study revealed this data:[21]

	Age Group			
Country	**18-29**	**30-49**	**50+**	**Total**
Turkey	9	7	10	26
Egypt	3	2	3	8
Jordan	5	1	1	7
Lebanon	27	17	10	54
Palestine	5	3	--	8
Tunisia	3	2	1	6
Indonesia	4	2	3	9
Malaysia	7	10	11	28
Pakistan	2	2	2	6
Senegal	5	2	2	9

Table 2: Percentage that believe homosexuality should be accepted

These are troubling numbers. There are a lot of minds to shift in most of these countries, and that won't happen overnight. But there are also glimmers of hope. The numbers are much better in America, where 52 percent of Muslims agree that homosexuality should be accepted. There are quite a few coming out stories online for gay Muslims in the US that turned out well. Depending on where you live, support groups may exist specifically for gay Muslims. Check the appendix for more resources that may be available.

---

[21] "The Global Divide on Homosexuality," Pew Research Center, June 4, 2013, www.pewglobal.org/2013/06/04/the-global-divide-on-homosexuality/.

Misogyny and Homosexuality

There is a sacred temple in southern India called the Sabarimala Temple. Women between the ages of ten and fifty have not been allowed into the temple for centuries, as they were considered of menstruating age. In 1991, a high court ruled that the ban was allowed and enforceable with police force. On September 28, 2018, the Supreme Court of India overturned that decision, saying that the ban was not an "essential" part of Hinduism. The ruling touched on an essential point about religion and freedom:

> "Any relationship with the Creator is a transcendental one crossing all socially created artificial barriers and not a negotiated relationship bound by terms and conditions. Such a relationship and expression of devotion cannot be circumscribed by dogmatic notions of biological or physiological factors arising out of rigid socio-cultural attitudes which do not meet the constitutionally prescribed tests. Patriarchy in religion cannot be permitted to trump over the element of pure devotion borne out of faith and the freedom to practice and profess one's religion. The subversion and repression of women under the garb of biological or physiological factors cannot be given the seal of legitimacy. Any rule based on discrimination or segregation of women pertaining to biological characteristics is not only unfounded, indefensible, and implausible but can also never pass the muster of constitutionality."[22]

Since the ruling, several women have attempted to enter and have been met with angry mobs attempting to prevent entry. This prompted an estimated 3.5 to 5 million women to join hands in India in a line stretching 385 miles in a protest to raise awareness for equality.[23]

Hinduism isn't alone in having patriarchal religious practices and teachings. It's difficult to read the Bible or the

---

[22] Indian Young Lawyers Association & Ors. v. The State of Kerala & Ors., Supreme Court of India, docket no. 373 of 2006, September 28, 2018, www.sci.gov.in/supremecourt/2006/18956/18956_2006_Judgement_28-Sep-2018.pdf.

[23] Kamala Thiagarajan, "Millions of Women in India Join Hands to Form a 385-Mile Wall of Protest," National Public Radio, January 4, 2019, www.npr.org/sections/goatsandsoda/2019/01/04/681988452/millions-of-women-in-india-join-hands-to-form-a-385-mile-wall-of-protest.

Qur'an and not immediately note the very clear message that being a woman is somehow *less* than being a man. Women are not usually spoken of or treated as equals, and they are usually not allowed to serve as religious leaders.

This patriarchal view in religion creates an inferiority not only for women but also for men who take the role of women in sex. This is not purely an objection to same-sex attraction—there is usually nary a mention of lesbianism in most religious texts. Historically, men who play the active role are respected and men in the passive role are despised—a view still held in Latino culture, among others. Homosexuality was viewed not so much as a violation of nature, but as a degradation of the male. It was also seen as a "waste" of seed (semen) in the purely procreative nature of sex, a topic we'll touch on in more detail shortly.

In classical Islamic poetry or prose of the eighth century, whether in Arabic or Persian, there was an acceptance of man/boy sexual relations. Setting aside the age difference for a moment, the important distinction is the parallels to women:

> "It was assumed that many, or indeed most, mature men would be sexually attracted to adolescent boys, in a way strictly parallel to— and compatible with—their attraction to women. Like women, such boys have hairless bodies and soft skin, and like them they are subordinate members of society, that is, subordinate to mature men."[24]

It was assumed that these older men would take the active role in sex, with the younger male being submissively passive.

> "While it was recognized that there *were* mature men who sought out the passive role in homosexual intercourse, they were viewed as both sick and contemptible; and indeed to accuse a mature man of such proclivities was both one of the strongest and one of the most common forms of insult." (Rowson)

As we are about to embark on the journey of looking at specific Biblical passages that are often used against homosexuality, please ask yourself if they seem like the words of

---

[24] E. K. Rowson, "Homosexuality ii. in Islamic Law," *Encyclopædia Iranica*, XII/4, pp. 441-445, http://www.iranicaonline.org/articles/homosexuality-ii.

a universally loving God of all of His creations or the work of men who viewed women as subordinate property whose main role was to serve men. I'd like to close this section with another quote from the Supreme Court of India ruling:

> "It is a universal truth that faith and religion do not countenance discrimination, but religious practices are sometimes seen as perpetuating patriarchy, thereby negating the basic tenets of faith and of gender equality and rights. The societal attitudes, too, center and revolve around the patriarchal mindset, thereby derogating the status of women in the social and religious milieu. All religions are simply different paths to reach the Universal One. Religion is basically a way of life to realize one's identity with the Divinity. However, certain dogmas and exclusionary practices and rituals have resulted in incongruities between the true essence of religion or faith and its practice that has come to be permeated with patriarchal prejudices. Sometimes, in the name of essential and integral facet of the faith, such practices are zealously propagated."[25]

It is my sincere belief that this is equally applicable to homosexuals for the same reasons.

Citing with Ignorance

"Both read the Bible day and night, but thou read black where I read white."

– William Blake

There is a meme that is widely circulated on the Internet showing a closeup of a man's arm tattoo (search "Leviticus tattoo meme" and you should find it easily). The man in the photo was interviewed as part of a news story about a gay man who was brutally attacked. He was a friend of one of the attackers and proudly showed off his tattoo for the cameras. While the crime his friend committed is no laughing matter, the man pictured has become the laughingstock of many social networks. His tattoo cites Leviticus 18:22. "Thou shall not lie with a male as one does with a woman. It is an abomination." The irony is that Leviticus

---

[25] Supreme Court of India, 4.

19:28 emphatically forbids tattoos: "Ye shall not make any cuttings in your flesh for the dead, nor print any marks upon you: I am the LORD."

The word "ignorance" doesn't mean lack of intelligence. It simply means "a lack of knowledge." There is nothing inherently wrong with a lack of knowledge, but there is something very wrong with citing a book you are ignorant about as a justification to harm someone else or to fight to deprive them of rights.

Reverend Mel White says that Bible ignorance is an epidemic in the United States:

> "Many folks who use the Bible to condemn homosexuality have never really studied the verses they cite. According to a study quoted by Dr. Peter Gomes in *The Good Book*, thirty-eight percent of Americans polled were certain the Old Testament was written a few years after Jesus's death. Ten percent believed Joan of Arc was Noah's wife. Many even thought the epistles were the wives of the apostles."[26]

As Reverend Dr. Laurence C. Keene says, "There's nothing wrong with a fifth-grade understanding of God . . . if you're in the fifth grade." The problem is that most Christians haven't really read the Bible. Reading the Bible and really understanding the words requires hard work and, in some cases, a lifetime of it. Keene adds, "When someone says to me, 'This is what the Bible says,' my response to them is, 'No, that is what the Bible *reads*. It is the struggle to understand context and language and culture and custom that helps us to understand the meaning or what it is saying.'"[27] [emphasis added]

How many people not only read the words in religious texts but also understand the original ancient languages they were written in? How many understand the historical culture of the authors who wrote them, or the men who translated them from language to language over the centuries? I would think there is no

---

[26] Mel White, "What the Bible Says—and Doesn't Say—about Homosexuality," accessed December 30, 2018, https://melwhite.org/bible-says-homosexuality/.

[27] *For the Bible Tells Me So*, directed by Daniel G. Karslake, First Run Features, 2007.

more egregious a way to dishonor any scripture than to cite it out of context to suit your own belief structure. Context doesn't just mean knowing the words and paragraphs surrounding what you're citing, it also means understanding the time period and the culture that it was written in. As we just learned, that context often reveals a diminished, submissive view of women. Men who acted like women were treated even worse than women.

In our increasingly busy lives, it is much easier to leave religious interpretations up to church leaders, and I believe that is very dangerous. The people who do these interpretations are essentially wielding the power of God's word like a weapon—often a weapon that has been used to target just about every kind of minority that has ever existed historically—from women to black people to homosexuals.

Biblical Literalists

People who quote ancient scripture, against gays or otherwise, are called "Biblical literalists." As we'll soon see, however, they are careful to "literally" follow only the teachings that are convenient to them. Through the use of confirmation bias we've been discussing, human beings tend to filter out information that contradicts their beliefs and lend more credibility than is warranted to information that confirms those beliefs—a bias toward confirmation. The more deeply held these beliefs, the more effort that goes into both finding sources to back up those beliefs and ignoring any sources that refute them. If you begin with a belief, perhaps instilled at an early age by parents or preachers, that homosexuality is yucky, what are the odds that you're going to keep reading Leviticus after 18:22 and decide to question the whole thing when you get to the tattoo part? If you believe that God created Adam and Eve six thousand years ago, what is the chance that you're going to read about the latest fossil digs that unearthed early human ancestor remains which were determined to be 3.2 million years old using argon-argon radiometric dating methods, or that you'd even care to understand what that method of dating is and how reliable it is?

Biblical literalism requires a somewhat intentional avoidance of facts. I'd like to tell you that these facts are getting harder and harder to avoid in the Information Age, but Google is both our friend and our enemy in this case. Google's algorithm is not programmed to favor facts; it's programmed to favor links from other sites. It is therefore possible to use Google to find information that justifies just about any position with more than a few proponents. Beliefs are strong, and if your life's moral structure was built upon them, allowing one of them to fall prey to facts can, like the single thread pulled from a sweater, cause the entire thing to unravel, which could result in a real crisis of identity for some people. It's no wonder that people cling so strongly to their beliefs. As writer Saul Bellow once said, "A great deal of intelligence can be invested in ignorance when the need for illusion is deep."

One of the most challenging aspects of my dealings with religious folks about homosexuality is the tendency of many of them to selectively interpret the Bible to suit their beliefs. If the believer enjoys the behavior in question, the section of the Bible that forbids it is either forgotten or interpreted into oblivion. If the behavior is appalling to the believer, the chapter and verse is recalled verbatim and quoted in front of as many television cameras as possible. By anyone's definition of hypocrisy, this is it.

The man with the tattoo believed so strongly that gays are bad, he cherry-picked a citation from Leviticus that he believed confirmed his bias without reading onward to see that getting his tattoo was also forbidden in Leviticus. Not to mention, he never made it to the New Testament where Jesus says:

> "Do not judge, or you too will be judged. For in the same way you judge others, you will be judged, and with the measure you use, it will be measured to you.
>
> Why do you look at the speck of sawdust in your brother's eye and pay no attention to the plank in your own eye? How can you say to your brother, 'Let me take the speck out of your eye,' when all the time there is a plank in your own eye? You hypocrite, first take the plank out of your own eye, and then you will see clearly to remove the speck from your brother's eye." (Matthew 7:1-5)

Speaking of hypocrisy, Jesus has a reputation for being loving and understanding, but if there's one thing He seemed to judge pretty harshly, it was hypocrisy. He condemned it more than anything else, and Paul echoed His words most accurately:

> "You, therefore, have no excuse, you who pass judgment on someone else, for at whatever point you judge the other, you are condemning yourself, because you who pass judgment do the same things." (Romans 2:1)

Leviticus 18:22 has the rule; Leviticus 20:13 outlines the punishment:

> "If a man lies with a man as one lies with a woman, both of them have done what is detestable. They must be put to death; their blood will be on their own heads." (Leviticus 20:13)

A bit of knowledge about historical context can really help here. When Leviticus was written (between 1440 and 1400 B.C.— that's fourteen hundred years before Christ was born, or over 3,400 years ago), the entire planet's population was an estimated fifty million,[28] and those people were not world travelers so it's doubtful that inhabitants at the time had any idea that it was even that many. It was a planet where the average life expectancy was twenty-nine.[29] The survival and propagation of the human species required procreation. Guidance to the masses in this time would have surely encouraged all sexual acts that would result in childbirth and discouraged all that did not. In fact, in Genesis 38:8-10, we learn that even pulling out before climax was punishable by death:

> "Then Judah said to Onan, 'Sleep with your brother's wife and fulfill your duty to her as a brother-in-law to raise up offspring for

---

[28] Colin McEvedy and Richard M. Jones, *Atlas of World Population History* (New York: Penguin Books, 1979):344.

[29] Oded Galor and Omer Moav, "Natural Selection and the Evolution of Life Expectancy," Minerva Center for Economic Growth, October 12, 2005, sticerd.lse.ac.uk/seminarpapers/dg09102006.pdf.

your brother.' But Onan knew that the child would not be his; so whenever he slept with his brother's wife, he spilled his semen on the ground to keep from providing offspring for his brother. What he did was wicked in the Lord's sight; so the Lord put him to death also."

So, taken in context, Leviticus is just another in a string of "rules" (also known as "Holiness Code") that seem to be intended to prolong life and encourage propagation of the species. This is hardly applicable to our resource starved, over-populated planet today. Most anti-homosexual folks stop at Leviticus 20:13, but we need to press on because there are some interesting prohibitions in that area of the Bible.

"Anyone who curses their father or mother is to be put to death. Because they have cursed their father or mother, their blood will be on their own head." (Leviticus 20:9)

Most teenagers would be put to death for this by the time they're fifteen.

"If a man commits adultery with another man's wife—with the wife of his neighbor—both the adulterer and the adulteress must be put to death." (Leviticus 20:10)

An estimated 20 percent of married men and 13 percent of married women would be put to death if this were enforced.[30]

"If a man has sexual relations with his father's wife, he has dishonored his father. Both the man and the woman are to be put to death; their blood will be on their own heads." (Leviticus 20:11)

"If a man sleeps with his daughter-in-law, both of them must be put to death. What they have done is a perversion; their blood will be on their own heads." (Leviticus 20:12)

"If a man has sexual relations with an animal, he is to be put to death, and you must kill the animal." (Leviticus 20:15)

---

[30] Wendy Wang, "Who Cheats More? The Demographics of Infidelity in America," Institute for Family Studies, January, 10, 2018, ifstudies.org/blog/who-cheats-more-the-demographics-of-cheating-in-america.

> "If a woman approaches an animal to have sexual relations with it, kill both the woman and the animal. They are to be put to death; their blood will be on their own heads." (Leviticus 20:16)

Isn't it interesting that the man has to *do it*, but the woman only needs to *approach*? That is an example of how women were viewed as less than men.

It was one of the laws of Leviticus that was responsible for the death of Jesus:

> "[A]nyone who blasphemes the name of the LORD must be put to death." (Leviticus 24:16)

By claiming he was the Son of God, he was convicted under this law as was explained in John 19:6-7:

> "As soon as the chief priests and their officials saw [Jesus], they shouted, 'Crucify! Crucify!' But Pilate answered, 'You take him and crucify him. As for me, I find no basis for a charge against him.' The Jewish leaders insisted, 'We have a law, and according to that law he must die, because he claimed to be the Son of God.'"

Lastly, there's the whole shellfish thing . . .

> "And all that have not fins and scales in the seas, and in the rivers, of all that move in the waters, and of any living thing which is in the waters, they shall be an abomination unto you." (KJV Leviticus 11:10)

Have you ever been to a crab or shrimp feed fund-raiser at a church? Those who cite Leviticus against homosexuals should either explain why that particular Leviticus citation is still applicable while all of these other citations are not, admit that they're cherry-picking the Bible to suit their own opinions, or consider that they're operating with cognitive dissonance.

The Sin of Sodom

"And sin, young man, is when you treat people like things."

– Terry Pratchett

The story of Sodom and Gomorrah is traditionally central to Jewish, Christian, and Muslim condemnation of homosexuality. The English origin of the word "sodomy" comes from the name of the town. In the Qur'an, the main character is named Lut (vs. Lot in the Christian version). The Arabic term for homosexual anal intercourse, *liwat*, comes from his name.[31]

If the story is read without context, one can only imagine that there must have been a giant gay fest going on in Sodom to become the moniker for homosexual sex.

> "Now the men of Sodom were wicked and were sinning greatly against the Lord." (Genesis 13:13)

> "Then the Lord said, 'The outcry against Sodom and Gomorrah is so great and their sin so grievous that I will go down and see if what they have done is as bad as the outcry that has reached me. If not, I will know.'" (Genesis 18:20–21)

> "The two angels arrived at Sodom in the evening, and Lot was sitting in the gateway of the city. When he saw them, he got up to meet them and bowed down with his face to the ground. 'My lords,' he said, 'please turn aside to your servant's house. You can wash your feet and spend the night and then go on your way early in the morning.'
> 'No,' they answered, 'we will spend the night in the square.' But he insisted so strongly that they did go with him and entered his house. He prepared a meal for them, baking bread without yeast, and they ate.
> Before they had gone to bed, all the men from every part of the city of Sodom—both young and old—surrounded the house. They called to Lot, 'Where are the men who came to you tonight? Bring them out to us so that we can have sex with them.'" (Genesis 19:1–5)

Could it be that rape, not consensual sex is what's wrong here? Historically speaking, there was also great sin in inhospitality—especially in these desert regions. To deny a traveler food or water or to take advantage of a traveler in a violent way was a sin second only to murder. Let's continue:

---

[31] Christopher van der Krogt, "Friday Essay: The Qur'an, the Bible, and Homosexuality in Islam," *The Conversation*, accessed January 6, 2019, theconversation.com/friday-essay-the-quran-the-bible-and-homosexuality-in-islam-61012.

> "Lot went outside to meet them and shut the door behind him and said, 'No, my friends. Don't do this wicked thing. Look, I have two daughters who have never slept with a man. Let me bring them out to you, and you can do what you like with them. But don't do anything to these men, for they have come under the protection of my roof.'" (Genesis 19:6–8)

Lot decides to offer this riotous crowd (of men, women, and children) his two virgin daughters in order to save his guests, apparently deducing that his daughters being raped would be preferable to his guests. The angels blind the mob, pull Lot into the house, send him and his family on their way, destroy Sodom and Gomorrah, and later turn Lot's wife into a pillar of salt because she looks back against the angels' orders.

Nowhere in the remainder of the Bible—Old or New Testament—is the sin of Sodom defined as sex between consenting male adults. Here are the sins of Sodom according to no less an authority than God Himself:

> "Now this was the sin of your sister Sodom: She and her daughters were arrogant, overfed, and unconcerned; they did not help the poor and needy. They were haughty and did detestable things before me. Therefore, I did away with them as you have seen." (Ezekiel 16:49–50)

I find it quite troubling when anyone who claims to be influenced by the story of Sodom and Gomorrah simply glosses over the part where God says their sins included not helping the poor and the needy. Surely that should be included equally as "detestable things." Remember the hospitality thing I mentioned before? Each time Jesus mentions Sodom and Gomorrah he does so in connection with inhospitality:

> "If anyone will not welcome you or listen to your words, leave that home or town and shake the dust off your feet. Truly I tell you, it will be more bearable for Sodom and Gomorrah on the day of judgment than for that town." (Matthew 10:14–15)

Later, in the New Testament, Sodom and Gomorrah is revisited:

> "Even as Sodom and Gomorrah, and the cities about them in like manner, giving themselves over to fornication, and going after

strange flesh, are set forth for an example, suffering the vengeance of eternal fire." (KJV Jude 7)

It's important that I use the King James Version here because there is mention of "strange flesh" that many novices assume means man-on-man sex. However, even many anti-gay heterosexual Christian scholars agree that the correct interpretation of "strange flesh" is Angel (non-human) flesh. Therefore, the sin of Sodom, as it relates to sex, is the desire of men to have sex with angels, not to have sex with other men.[32] A helpful list of twelve of these scholars and their interpretations of Jude 6-8 is linked at oktobegaybook.com, or you can visit the site directly at www.gaychristian101.com/Jude.html#placename

According to Methodist pastor Dr. Edward Bauman:

> "The real irony is that homosexuals have been the victim of inhospitality for thousands of years in the Christian nations of the world. Condemned by the church and the state, they have been ridiculed, rejected, persecuted, and even executed. In the name of an erroneous interpretation of the crime of Sodom, the true crime of Sodom has been continuously perpetrated to our own day."[33]

In other words, those who preach that Sodom and Gomorrah is about homosexuality, and who use those beliefs to persecute gays are missing the big lesson from the story. Any time someone who is different is scorned or made to feel unwelcome, those being scornful and rude have committed the sins of Sodom.

---

[32] Rick Brentlinger, "Does Jude Condemn Gays?" GayChristian101, June 16, 2017, http://www.gaychristian101.com/Jude.html.

[33] Edward Bauman, quoted in Peter McWilliams, *Ain't Nobody's Business If You Do: The Absurdity of Consensual Crimes in a Free Society* (Los Angeles: Prelude, 1993): 616.

Jesus and the New Testament

"I hope we never get to the point that we put ourselves in Jesus's place. But when I read the New Testament basically, we get three mandates: to love God, to love each other, and to take care of the least among us. And I think this is at least a step in the right direction."

– Bob Riley

Much of the material we've been looking at up to now comes from the Old Testament. Many Christians (especially in the "hate the sin, not the sinner" camp) are quick to point out that modern churches have mostly moved off of the Old Testament teachings in favor of the New Testament. I consider this a giant step in the right direction since Jesus mostly taught love, compassion, and understanding. Yet even with these more love-based teachings, people still find ways to discriminate against homosexuals. In fact, many religious folks seem to cling to Old Testament teachings only about the topic of homosexuality. I prefer to refer to them as "Leviticans," a term coined by writer John Scalzi in his "Whatever" blog entry by the same name:

> "To suggest that a Christian is actually a Levitican is not to say he or she is false in faith—rather, it is to suggest that their faith is elsewhere in the Bible, in the parts that are easy to understand: the rules, the regulations, all the things that are clear cut about what you can do and what you can't do to be right with God. Rules are far easier to follow than Christ's actual path, which needs humility and sacrifice and the ability to forgive, love and cherish even those who you oppose and who oppose and hate you."[34]

Entire books have been written to discuss the New Testament with regards to homosexuality, but we should do at least a cursory exploration of the relevant paragraphs in the interest of balance lest I be accused of misrepresenting Christianity by using tactics of selective quoting. Fair warning that this can get a little esoteric, so bear with me.

---

[34] John Scalzi, "Leviticans," *Whatever* (blog), February 24, 2004, http://whatever.scalzi.com/2004/02/24/leviticans/.

The New Testament has three passages that refer directly to what we modern humans would call homosexual activity. Let's discuss them in turn:

> "Because of this, God gave them over to shameful lusts. Even their women exchanged natural sexual relations for unnatural ones. In the same way the men also abandoned natural relations with women and were inflamed with lust for one another. Men committed shameful acts with other men and received in themselves the due penalty for their error." (Romans 1:26-27)

Romans 1 is Paul's theology. It is written to a Jewish audience since he refers to gentiles as "they" and "them." Paul believed that gentile ethnic impurity was based upon idolatry (the worship of idols), and he uses Romans 1 to discuss the origins and consequences of idolatry. You'll note the beginning of verse 26 begins with "Because of this." Verse 25 defines "this":

> "They exchanged the truth about God for a lie and worshiped and served created things rather than the Creator—who is forever praised. Amen." (Romans 1:25)

It's fairly clear that Paul is saying that God "gave them over" to shameful lusts as punishment for idolatry. Paul was giving the Christians in Rome a laundry list, which included the various examples of unnatural behavior. His message was "Once you know God and you turn from God, woe unto you," not "Homosexuality is bad."[35] Anita Cadonau-Huseby, a religious scholar and blogger, said it best when she broke down the history and context of Romans in her blog post entitled "Romans 1: Read the Whole Chapter, Kiddo":

> "We need to be honest enough to say we don't know exactly what Paul meant or what Paul might have thought concerning our current day understanding of homosexuality. We know, however, that Paul was a Jew and that the emphasis on purity in Leviticus were part

---

[35] Peter McWilliams, "Ain't Nobody's Business If You Do: The Absurdity of Consensual Crimes in a Free Society," DrugSense.org
http://www.drugsense.org/mcwilliams/www.mcwilliams.com/books/books/aint/3090.htm.

of Paul's thinking, as was the Greco-Roman worldview in which he lived."[36]

Let's move on to Corinthians and Timothy.

> "Or do you not know that wrongdoers will not inherit the kingdom of God? Do not be deceived: neither the sexually immoral, nor idolaters, nor adulterers, nor men who have sex with men, nor thieves, nor the greedy, nor drunkards, nor slanderers, nor swindlers will inherit the kingdom of God." (1 Corinthians 6:9-10)

> "We also know that the law is made not for the righteous but for lawbreakers and rebels, the ungodly and sinful, the unholy and irreligious, for those who kill their fathers or mothers, for murderers, for the sexually immoral, for those practicing homosexuality, for slave traders and liars and perjurers—and for whatever else is contrary to the sound doctrine." (1 Timothy 1:9-10)

The Bible was not originally written in English. The New Testament was written almost entirely in Greek. Over time, these texts have been translated to many languages, and because there are different interpretations of these languages, there are different versions of the Bible. Corinthians and Timothy represent Paul's letters to the city of Corinth and to Timothy, Paul's younger colleague.

The words "men who have sex with men" in Corinthians and "those practicing homosexuality" in Timothy are both translations of the Greek word *arsenokoitai*. The word is rarely used, and its exact meaning is not known for certain. But historically, we know that Paul had rabbinical training, so he would be very familiar with Leviticus (written in Hebrew). Paul did not understand Hebrew, but he relied upon a third century B.C. Greek translation of the Hebrew Scriptures called the Septuagint.

During Paul's time, he would have known homosexual behavior as the Greek word *paiderasste*, but he didn't use that word. Instead, it appears that what he did was coin a new word

---

[36] Anita Cadonau-Huseby, "05. Romans 1: Read the Whole Chapter, Kiddo (blog post)," Christian Gays Articles & Resources, 2010, accessed December 30, 2018, resources.christiangays.com/05-romans-1-read-the-whole-chapter-kiddo/.

from the Greek translation of Leviticus 20:13 contained in the Septuagint. The Greek translation of that verse is roughly *hos an koimethe meta arsenos koiten gunaikos* (And not lie-down with mankind [in] beds [of] a woman/wife).

Paul appears to have combined the noun *arseno* with the Greek verb *koiten* into a new word. His audience would have been familiar with Leviticus also, so they would not have needed an explanation of the new word for an old idea (temple prostitution). Over time, Christians extended the meaning of *arsenokoites* to cover other behaviors they found objectionable. It's safe to say that the meaning and translation have changed over time.[37]

Leaders Who Need to Be Led Instead

"People should not be surprised when a morally offensive lifestyle is physically attacked."

– Pope Benedict XVI

Shortly after midnight on October 7, 1998, a twenty-one-year-old young man named Matthew Shepard met Aaron McKinney and Russell Henderson at the Fireside Lounge in Laramie, Wyoming. McKinney and Henderson offered Shepard a ride in their car. After Shepard said that he was gay, the two men robbed, pistol-whipped, tortured, and tied him to a fence in a remote, rural area, leaving him to die. Still tied to the fence, Shepard was discovered eighteen hours later by Aaron Kreifels, who initially mistook Shepard for a scarecrow.

Shepard was in a coma. He had suffered fractures to the back of his head and in front of his right ear. He experienced severe brain-stem damage, which affected his body's ability to regulate heart rate, body temperature, and other vital functions.

---

[37] Sean Isler, "1 Corinthians 6:9-10 and 1 Timothy 1:9-11," *Bible Abuse Directed at Homosexuals*, St. John's MCC Community Website, updated February 3, 2012, www.stopbibleabuse.org/biblical-references/paul/corinthians-and-timothy.html.

There were also about a dozen small lacerations around his head, face, and neck. His injuries were deemed too severe for doctors to operate. He never regained consciousness and remained on full life support. While he lay in intensive care, the people of Laramie held candlelight vigils.

Shepard was pronounced dead at 12:53 a.m. on October 12, 1998, at Poudre Valley Hospital in Fort Collins, Colorado. Police arrested McKinney and Henderson shortly thereafter, finding the bloody gun and Shepard's shoes and wallet in their truck.

After Shepard's death, a pastor in North Carolina published an open letter regarding the trial of Aaron McKinney that read:

> "Gays are under the death penalty. His blood is guilty before God (Leviticus 20:13). If a person kills a gay, the gay's blood is upon the gay and not upon the hands of the person doing the killing. The acts of gays are so abominable to God. His Word is there, and we can't change it."[38]

This pastor used this Leviticus citation to blame Matthew Shepard for his own murder. In 2012, a pastor named Charles L. Worley of Providence Road Baptist Church called for gays and lesbians to be put in an electrified pen and ultimately killed off. "Build a great big, large fence—150 or 100 miles long—put all the lesbians in there. Do the same thing for the queers and the homosexuals and have that fence electrified so they can't get out. […] You know what? In a few years, they'll die out. Do you know why? They can't reproduce!"[39]

The most recent example of this at the time of writing this book was the mass shooting at Pulse, a gay nightclub in Orlando, Florida. Forty-nine people lost their lives in the (at the time) deadliest mass shooting in US history when a man with a gun

---

[38] Mel White, "What the Bible Says—and Doesn't Say—about Homosexuality," accessed December 30, 2018, https://melwhite.org/bible-says-homosexuality/.

[39] "Local Pastor Calls for Death of 'Queers & Homosexuals,'" YouTube video, speech by Charles L. Worley, 2012, retrieved January 20, 2019 from www.youtube.com/watch?feature=player_embedded&v=d2n7vSPwhSU.

went on a shooting spree on June 12, 2016. The killer pledged allegiance to ISIS, an Islamic terrorist organization, just before the shooting. It's very important to note that doesn't mean ISIS was responsible for the killings. Anyone can claim allegiance to anything before they commit a crime. It does speak to the idea that impressionable sociopaths are often influenced by radical religious teachers to do terrible acts.

It's worth noting that shortly after the Florida shooting, Pastor Roger Jimenez of Verity Baptist Church in Sacramento, California, gave the following sermon to his congregation:[40]

> "Are you sad that fifty pedophiles were killed today? Um no. I think that's great. I think that helps society. I think Orlando, Florida, is a little safer tonight. The tragedy is that more of them didn't die. The tragedy is I'm kind of upset he didn't finish the job—because these people are predators. They are abusers. I wish the government would round them all up, put them up against a firing wall, put the firing squad in front of them, and blow their brains out."

As I write this, he is still the active pastor at that church.

As a society, when we don't take people like this to task, we perpetuate their bias. That bias kills and hurts others. Bullies and sociopaths hear religious leaders speak like this and feel empowered to hurt or kill gay people. When we witness someone being bullied and we don't defend the victim, we're siding with the bully—even when that bully is a religious leader.

If, as citizens of a planet we all must share, we don't see our connectedness and similarities instead of our differences, more innocent, loving people will die. Allowing individuals like these people to stand up and call themselves religious at all, never mind religious *leaders*, is dangerous to all of us.

---

[40] Tom Parfitt, "'It's a tragedy more didn't die' Hate preacher's sick speech on Orlando attack sparks fury" https://www.express.co.uk/news/world/679923/Roger-Jimenez-Orlando-shooting-ISIS-Islamic-State-Omar-Mateen

The Power of God

"I cannot imagine a God who rewards and punishes the objects of his creation and is but a reflection of human frailty."

– Albert Einstein

"I can't, for the life of me, imagine that God would say, 'I will punish you because you are black; you should have been white. I will punish you because you are a woman; you should have been a man. I punish you because you are homosexual; you ought to have been heterosexual. I can't for the life of me believe that that is how God sees things."

– Reverend Desmond Tutu

Many Christians believe in a god that can create an entire planet and all the life on it in seven days. A god who is so powerful that he could prevent me from typing this very sentence if He so chose. Yet this powerful god is unable or unwilling to stop me from being gay? If God so disapproves of homosexuality, why have it at all? Religious folks usually come back with one of two answers:

1. Homosexuality is the work of the devil, and we need to resist it.
2. God grants us all free will, and we need to choose to follow his guidance on our own rather than be forced.

If the sins in the Bible are the devil's temptation, is everyone who has ever cursed at their parent destined to join me in hell? As for free will, is it really free will if the punishment for choosing incorrectly lands you in a pit of fire for all of eternity? What kind of choice is that?

The Bible has been used to justify everything from slavery to murder. Things we'd all agree today are absolutely horrific. If you were a God-fearing slave owner in the early 1800s and you faced the judgment of God upon your death, should He give you a pass on hell because you contorted the Bible to justify your ownership of slaves, as many "Christian" slave owners did during that period? Would the people who stoned a child to death for being "stubborn and rebellious" in 1400 BC be sent to heaven because Deuteronomy 21:18-21 told them to, while the woman in Tyler, Texas, who bashed in her sons' heads with heavy rocks in 2004 because she thought the Lord told her to do is sent to hell for murder?[41]

I suppose it boils down to what kind of god you think God is. If you believe the words of the Bible, you need to come to terms with how brutal the punishments were for things we'd consider fairly minor flubs today. As the Freedom from Religion website says, "Far from protecting the sanctity of life, the Bible promotes capital punishment for conduct which no civilized person or nation would regard as criminal."[42]

There are so many ways to have your murder be a justified homicide in the eyes of God. Let's name off a few:

- Lying about virginity (Deuteronomy 22:20-21)
- Sleeping with an engaged woman who doesn't scream for help (Deuteronomy 22:23-27)
- Having sex with your daughter-in-law (Leviticus 20:12),
- Having sex with a man if you're a man (Leviticus 20:13)
- Marrying a woman and her daughter (Leviticus 20:14)
- Breaking the Sabbath (Exodus 31:14, Numbers 15:32-36)
- Trying to convert people to another religion (Deuteronomy 13:1-11, Deuteronomy 18:20)
- Striking (Exodus 21:15), cursing (Exodus 21:17, Leviticus 20:9), or being stubborn with your parents (Deuteronomy 21:18-21)

With so many ways to be justifiably killed by your peers, it's amazing that we're here at all as a species in the twenty-first century! Why would God—who is all-knowing and presumably a master of communication—do such a poor and conflicting job of

---

[41] Associated Press, "Trial Begins for Mom Who Stoned Sons to Death," *Fox News*, updated January 14, 2015, www.foxnews.com/story/trial-begins-for-mom-who-stoned-sons-to-death.

[42] "What Does the Bible Say about Abortion?" Freedom from Religion Foundation, accessed December 30, 2018, ffrf.org/outreach/item/18514-what-does-the-bible-say-about-abortion.

spelling out all the rules? Especially if the consequences for breaking them are so dire?

Handle Your Weapons with Care

Many books have been written about the biblical aspects of the homosexual debate, and if this is a big part of your issue related to your own homosexuality or the homosexuality of someone you love, you have an obligation to wield that with responsibility. It can be a tool that reminds you to be thankful and benevolent, or it can be a weapon used to strike at those you love. I hope what you've learned from this chapter is that there are thousands of years of human history between you and the source of these teachings. Thousands of years filled with flawed human beings who were struggling to explain a much worse existence than we have today. Some had good intentions; some were lost in power and ignorance. We have more resources at our fingertips than any society that has ever lived on this planet before us. I encourage you to use the thing God gave you to study your religion with: your brain. Don't surrender that effort to others, allowing them to tell you what your religion's text means. Especially if you're going to make decisions like whether or not to kick your gay child out onto the street—or worse.

It's useful to remember that Jesus modeled unconditional love in a way that few humans have since. Almost every religion reiterates the message of acceptance and love. It's time for us to step up as a species—no matter what our differences in skin color, sexual orientation, gender, or religion—to practice this teaching. The next section of the book is about doing just that.

Part Three: Accepting Others

"The ultimate lesson all of us have to learn is unconditional love, which includes not only others but ourselves as well."

– Elisabeth Kübler-Ross

Chapter 8: So, You Have a Gay Child

"I don't understand why people think that having a gay child means they failed as a parent. Disowning your gay child means you failed as a parent."

— Unknown

"Parenthood is about raising and celebrating the child you have, not the child you thought you'd have. It's about understanding your child is exactly the person they are supposed to be. And, if you're lucky, they might be the teacher who turns you into the person you're supposed to be."

— The Water Giver

If you happen to be reading this book because your son or daughter is gay, this chapter is for you. We're going to discuss exactly how you're to blame for all of this. I'm kidding, of course. Right off the bat, you'll be pleased to know that you had very little to do with your child's homosexuality. You may have influenced the amount of time it took for them to be honest with you about it, but let's not get ahead of ourselves. I'm hoping that by now you're becoming convinced that it's not a "flaw" in your child at all but instead is a natural expression of the wide spectrum of human sexuality.

Homosexuality is usually present from an early age, and any perceived delay you may have seen between your child being born and being gay is due to the normal human sexual development cycle coupled with his or her own growing understanding and how safe they felt telling you—and even themselves!

As a parent, you will either create a space for your child to feel safe to tell you the truth or you won't. The stakes couldn't be higher. Some of the most tragic stories I've heard are parents interviewed after their child commits suicide when they tearfully say, "I wish he would have told me what he was going through!" Make your home a safe place for them to be whoever they are and to tell you about it. We'll discuss how to do that in the sections that follow.

Homophobia and Bigotry

The word "homophobic" has become a bit overused. Homophobia literally means fear (phobia) of homosexuality. It does *not* mean hatred of homosexuality, as is the common use of the word these days. Part of the reason that the term has come to mean both "hate" and "fear" is because some people greatly dislike being scared and they lash out at what's scaring them. Fear is a sponsoring emotion for anger, so some people who are scared of homosexuality *demonstrate* that fear through hatred and anger. A former coworker of mine confessed that he would get very angry if someone he loved was injured. He told of a time that his wife had cut her finger badly with a knife. He explained that he started yelling at her about not being careful enough with the knife as she was standing there bleeding. Why? Because he was scared to see someone he loved in pain, and instead of exhibiting that fear, he exhibited the anger *about having* the fear. To an outside observer, it might seem like an irrational response or that he was being a jerk, but once you understand the underlying emotions, it makes more sense.

Sometimes anger is the only negative emotion people express because they see the world through a very limited set of emotions. Fear, sadness, and anger tend to blend together into anger. Happiness, joyfulness, celebration, and contentment tend to blend together into contentment. It is absolutely OK to go through your entire life this way as long as you don't want to understand what's behind your reactions, but you're probably reading this book because you *do* want to get that understanding. Without it, you may not understand why you think two guys holding hands or kissing stirs up such discomfort. In other words, when you ask gay people to "keep their business to themselves" you may be avoiding fear or discomfort.

Another word that is often overused or poorly applied is the word "bigot." A bigot is someone "who is strongly partial to one's own group (e.g., religion, race, gender, political party, etc.) and is intolerant of those who differ."[43] The key word there is "intolerant." Not everyone who opposes gay rights does so from a place of intolerance. They may truly have no animosity or anger towards gay people.

You might be wondering, "What difference does it make?" It matters. If I know someone is homophobic, my goal is to address their fears. If I know someone is a bigot, they likely perceive that my homosexuality means we have more differences than similarities when the opposite is likely true. If someone is neither but is still opposed to equal rights, I know that the discussion is purely a legal debate. Properly understanding the

---

[43] "Bigot," *Your Dictionary*, Love to Know, accessed January 21, 2019, www.yourdictionary.com/bigot.

objection is a huge step towards meeting it with a counter argument.

So, decide now if you are homophobic, a bigot, or neither of those—but be honest about it. You are the one working on you in this book. If you're afraid of homosexuality, it's up to *you* to figure out what's causing that fear. If you're angry or intolerant of gays, it's up to *you* to do the work to understand why.

Fear for Your Child's Safety

In the parent-child relationship, there is another obvious fear we should discuss, and that is a fear *for* your child. My mom fell into this category when I came out. She was worried about all kinds of things. Me getting HIV, homophobia in the world causing me discrimination or injury, etc. If this describes you, I strongly recommend that you attend some Parents and Friends of Lesbian and Gays (PFLAG) meetings. You will find a lot of parents in the same position, and their support will be very helpful. What I will say about it here is that it's important to challenge your fears and get facts. My mom was very concerned about me getting HIV and used to lecture me all the time about safer sex, but she never said a word to my straight older brother who was more sexually active than I was at the time. She figured HIV was only a gay disease (it's not). From a statistical risk standpoint, she was worried about the wrong son.

Be careful not to turn your fear for your child into a wedge that pushes them away. Sometimes parents respond to their fear *for* their child with threats *toward* their child. They think that what's needed is a little "tough love" to scare the gay out of their kid. This can take the form of everything from arguments to conversion therapy (discussed in the section that follows called "Gay Reparative Therapy") to shipping them off to religious "schools" in foreign countries. These parents aren't doing this because they hate their children; they're doing it because they love them and it feels like the most loving thing to do is to coerce them to change who they are. This is like sending your kid off to hard labor for having brown hair. They didn't choose it, it's not going to change, and they're being punished for it.

The worst part about these "remedies" in the name of love is that once you finally do figure out this whole thing in *your* head and come to accept and love your child for who they are, you may have immense guilt for the things you put them through while you were figuring it out, and they may have a lot of anger directed at you for it as well. They have their own challenges about being gay; try to avoid putting *your* issues about it on *them*. If you find yourself fearful of what might happen to your child and/or are embarrassed about their homosexuality, you should own that discomfort and work with support groups to get past it rather than attempting to change your child so that you can be comfortable.

You will be their parent for the rest of your life, but that is no guarantee that you will have any relationship with them until the end. The way you react to their sexuality now might affect your relationship with them for the rest of your life.

Creating a Safe Place to Come Out

If and when your child comes out of the closet is influenced by many factors. Here are just a few:

1. Geographic location
2. Level of demonstrated homophobia in the family
3. Level of demonstrated homophobia in social circles
4. Emotional strength of the gay person
5. Financial reliance on the family
6. Religious influence of the family
7. Political leanings of the family
8. Confidence in sexual orientation of the gay person
9. Perceived social safety of the gay person
10. Availability of confidantes
11. Communication skills of everyone involved

It's really important to see that these factors are not all controllable by you as a parent, but there are some crucial ones for you to pay attention to. If you or another family member says things like, "Look at that faggot" when a gay person pops up on the TV screen, or if that kind of comment is made by someone else and you say nothing, it is interpreted as agreement. Comments such as "If you ever turned out gay, I'd disown you" are not as uncommon as one might hope.

As I mentioned earlier, my uncle told me that AIDS was God's punishment to gays. I never forgot that. It was a serious obstacle to me telling him I was gay at twenty-two. He didn't remember even saying it when we talked about it after I came out. He told me he'd always love me no matter what, but it certainly wasn't the impression I'd operated under for the five years prior. My uncle has since passed away. He and I were close all the way to the end of his life, but that just made his off-handed remark even more impactful. To him, that comment was just a simple conversational remark. To me, it was devastating, and I carried it with me for years until I came out. Your words have meaning, and your lack of words have meaning. *Always remember that.*

The first step to making a safe environment for your child is for you to get the facts. One of this book's primary aims is to help you with this, so congratulations on taking this step. Once you have a firm grasp of the facts, have dispelled myths, and are becoming more comfortable with the thought of your child being gay, it's time to tell your son or daughter that you're a safe place to come for this news. If you know that homophobic comments were made, now is the time to set the record, um, straight, so to speak.

If you don't yet have your spouse on board, it is *your* responsibility to accomplish this. While it's true that your child has his/her own relationship with your spouse, your relationship with him or her is more equal from a power perspective. You need to take the time to work through any myths or misinformation they may be operating under and help them to gain comfort. If you have homophobic friends, it's time to let them know also. Your unsupportive or homophobic friends may cause you problems (see "Parents Have a Closet Too" below). Groups like PFLAG have chapters all across the country and can help you with some of these issues. You'll meet other parents struggling with the same things as well as supportive folks who've made it through the rough parts.

If you find out that your child is gay, you may suddenly conclude that you now have "nothing in common" or that your child's homosexuality is so different from your view of the world that you can't connect with them anymore. Nothing could be further from the truth. Your son's relationships with other boys or your daughter's relationships with other girls will share 90 percent of the experiences you had growing up. Those relationships will have infatuation, physical attraction, love, broken hearts, competition, rejection, and all the other parts of two humans relating to each other. Don't suddenly conclude that you will be unable to help them navigate these areas of life simply because their partner's gender is the same as their own. It is useful for you to remind your child of how much you will be able to relate to them. Let them know you're there for them just as you would be if they were straight. The differences that do exist between homosexual and heterosexual attraction are such a minor part of the whole process that they are simply not important. I have received and given excellent relationship advice from and to my straight friends *and* my gay friends.

Once you get comfortable with this idea, I'd like to remind you of one other aspect you may not have considered: every gay kid has to conquer the idea of coming out and gaining or losing their relationship with their family and friends. Not all of these are success stories. Consider that your son's boyfriends or daughter's girlfriends are potentially in a bad place with *their* families. Make sure your child knows that your house is a safe place for their gay friends. You may find it to be beneficial in your own journey to help a child that isn't your own through the experience with parents who may not be as accepting as you are. Many gay kids have "adopted" parents who are uncles, aunts, or friends' parents, and some even owe their lives to these connections.

Parents Have a Closet Too

One thing I often tell parents of gay children is that sometimes a child comes out of the closet and the parents go right in behind them. After I came out, my mom struggled a bit with the news. She was a hairstylist, and, in addition to her profession influencing her views about gays in general, she wasn't sure what to say when her clients—some of whom had been clients since I was a small child—asked how I was doing. They would ask, for example, if I was dating any nice girls yet. For a while, she avoided the topic completely.

My advice is to think about the situation like this: Would you rather impress upon your friends that you're a staunch opponent of homosexuals or that you love your child unconditionally? In my view, the latter is far more admirable. If you lose friends over the news, what those people are saying is that they'd rather be comfortable with their notions of homosexuality than support you in loving your child. In my view, those aren't friends, and I stand by that statement whether you're gay or straight.

I'd like you to consider the bravery your child has shown to come out to you. It will take bravery for you to come out about your child to your friends, family, and coworkers also. I strongly advise that you don't resist this. You will be surprised to hear how many others you know are in the same place with a son, daughter, niece, nephew, or sibling. My mom discovered that several of her longtime clients also had gay children. It was only after she opened up about me that she found out. Don't miss out on that support. If the relationships sour after you tell them, then were they worth saving? Shouldn't our friends love us for who we are? Shouldn't they hold us to higher versions of ourselves?

Gay Reparative Therapy

In October of 2012, California became the first state to make gay reparative therapy for minors illegal. As I write this, seventeen other states have passed similar laws since then.

Now may be a good time to make sure we're on the same page about what gay reparative therapy is, the techniques that are used, and the evidence that supports its ineffectuality.

Gay reparative therapy is highly controversial for many reasons, not the least of which is the name itself. "Reparative" leads one to believe that there is something to be "fixed" in the first place. "Fixing" sexuality is just as impossible and repugnant as "fixing" race or "fixing" height. Because of this, you may hear the process called "conversion therapy" instead. Don't fool yourself. The techniques used are the same regardless of the name. They are barbaric and naïve and are rarely practiced by licensed professionals.

Usually these conversion therapy centers are run from church-based organizations. Early processes involved electric shocks applied along with nausea-inducing drugs while erotic same-sex images were shown to the subject. This was meant to reduce the entirely involuntary and natural erection or physical stimulation caused by seeing such images. While there has been some success in suppressing this stimulation from same-sex images, *increasing* stimulation from opposite-sex images has never seen much success at all. In other words, *the subjects became involuntarily nonsexual, but that didn't change the fact that they were still attracted to the same gender.*

Douglas Haldeman writes in "Sexual Orientation Conversion Therapy for Gay Men and Lesbians: A Scientific Examination" that such methods applied to anyone except gay people would be called torture. He concludes, "Individuals undergoing such treatments do not emerge heterosexually inclined; rather they become shamed, conflicted, and fearful about their homosexual feelings."[44] Ask yourself if this is how

---

[44] Douglas C. Haldeman, "Sexual Orientation Conversion Therapy for Gay Men and Lesbians: A Scientific Examination," in John C. Gonsiorek and James D. Weinrich (eds.), *Homosexuality: Research Implications for Public Policy* (Thousand Oaks, CA: Sage Publications, 1991), 149-60, www.drdoughaldeman.com/doc/ScientificExamination.pdf.

you'd like your son or daughter to exist in the world for the rest of their life—even after you're gone.

You may hear of one or two "success" stories from these groups. People who claim to have completely transformed themselves from homosexual to heterosexual. But these are dubious claims. Often these subjects (mostly men) are married with children and find it easier to step into denial than face the loss of their families. Furthermore, as adults, we all choose our battles and make trade-offs. There are some gay men who perhaps have a low enough Kinsey number and want that "straight, normal" life so badly that they're willing to trade the work of fighting off natural urges. Many of these men become homophobic or take anti-gay political positions (a topic we'll cover in Chapter 10: Internalized Homophobia). These positions do the work of trying to convince themselves and others that the people involved really are Kinsey zeros when they most likely are not.

Truly confirming the effectiveness of changing orientation requires scientific rigor. The American Psychological Association (APA) did a review of the literature on this topic in 2009. They concluded that almost all of the studies reviewed failed to meet that scientific rigor. The APA concluded:

> "[E]nduring change to an individual's sexual orientation is uncommon. The participants in this body of research continued to experience same-sex attractions following SOCE [Sexual Orientation Change Efforts] and did not report significant change to other-sex attractions that could be empirically validated, though some showed lessened physiological arousal to sexual stimuli. Compelling evidence of decreased same-sex sexual behavior and of engagement in sexual behavior with the other sex was rare. Few studies provided strong evidence that any changes produced in laboratory conditions translated to daily life. Thus, the results of scientifically valid research indicate that it is unlikely that individuals will be able to reduce same-sex attractions or increase other-sex sexual attractions through SOCE."[45]

---

[45] Judith M. Glassgold et al., "Appropriate Therapeutic Responses to Sexual Orientation," American Psychological Association, August 2009, www.apa.org/pi/lgbt/resources/therapeutic-response.pdf.

What I again want to stress at this point is that being gay involves much more than sexual attraction. It involves emotional attraction, olfactory attraction (sense of smell), physical (nonsexual) attraction, and masculinity/femininity attraction. These various types of attractions are deeply woven into us as human beings. Assuming you're straight, consider how difficult it would be for you to change your attractions to the opposite gender. How deeply ingrained are those attractions in your life? When did you choose these attractions? Consider the people who catch your eye at parties or throughout your day. Imagine forcing your mind, body, and soul to react to the same gender instead. Hopefully that exercise in empathy will convince you to abandon any thoughts you have that your gay child could somehow be something they aren't.

Diversity

Before we go further, I want to revisit this concept of being "broken" in the first place. The world is an amazing place of diversity. As a species, we contribute to our continued existence and growth because of our diversity, not because of our sameness. Here is a partial list of some of the gay people who've helped to shape this planet by contributing to our civilization:

- Socrates, 400 B.C.
- Aristotle, 300 B.C.
- Alexander the Great, 300 B.C.
- Julius Caesar, 100 B.C.
- Pope Julius III, 1550-1555
- Leonardo da Vinci, 15th c.
- Michelangelo, 15th c.
- Ralph Waldo Emerson, 19th c.
- Oscar Wilde, 19th c.
- Eleanor Roosevelt, 19th c.
- Tchaikovsky, 19th c.
- Cole Porter, 20th c.
- Jane Addams, 20th c.

- Tennessee Williams, 20th c.
- Leonard Bernstein, 20th c.
- Alan Turing, 20th c.
- Malcolm Forbes, 20th c.
- Marlon Brando, 20th c.
- Andy Warhol, 20th c.
- James Dean, 20th c.
- Richard Chamberlain, 20th c.
- Johnny Mathis, 20th c.
- Sally Ride, 21st c.
- Ellen DeGeneres, 21st c.
- Tim Cook, 21st c.
- Rachel Maddow, 21st c.
- Martina Navratilova, 21st c.

There are thousands and thousands more. Can you imagine a world without these people's influences? Without their contributions? If you find computers to be helpful in your life, you can thank Alan Turing, as they might not exist today without him. Women's rights were greatly advanced by Jane Addams. Consider that your child has gifts and contributions for the world as well. His or her sexual orientation is almost certainly secondary to those contributions.

As you look at the list above, ask yourself if you remember these people as gay people or as the talented composers, authors, artists, engineers, inventors, actors, and philosophers that they were. Our sexual orientation is personally important but a small part of who we are to the world. I encourage you to keep this expanded perspective in mind about your own sexuality and that of your child.

What Support Looks Like

Supporting your gay child looks different depending on what phase of life they're currently in. This experience is cumulative, however. If your son or daughter is currently in adolescence, you may want to take a look at the sections about earlier stages of life to see if you can recall any experiences during those stages that you could discuss with them today.

Early Childhood

During my travels through life, I've heard from many gays who told me they were certain from a very early age that they were gay. Some just didn't feel right in the forced gender roles (i.e., boys would choose dolls over toy guns and vice versa for girls) or seemed to get along better with friends of the opposite gender. This anecdotal evidence should not be dismissed easily.

It's difficult to scientifically prove the age at which sexual orientation begins to manifest itself, but from the early age so many gays report experiencing homosexual thoughts, it's clearly long before it could be considered a socially influenced event. In fact, some parents spot the opposite-gender tendencies of their kids and try to force them to stop, chastising boys for playing with dolls or girls for playing cowboys and Indians.

Despite the efforts of these parents, their kids will still grow up with the orientation they have, it's just that they may have issues accepting it as a result of the judgment from their parents. They don't get to choose, and parents don't get to choose for them.

It's really important to know that the degree of masculinity or femininity that your son or daughter displays during early childhood has little bearing on what their sexuality will be as Mother Nature kicks in around puberty. There are feminine straight guys and tomboy straight girls. There are masculine gay guys and feminine lesbians. Some boys will play with dolls as young children and then grow up to be straight, and others will play with toy soldiers and grow up to be gay.

Being supportive at this age means you support their play style without judgment. Teach them that whatever toys they want to play with are fine with you. If they seem to get crushes on the same gender, or seem more interested in having opposite-gender playmates, your indifference about that is all they need from you to know that you love them unconditionally.

Adolescence

Adolescence can be one of the toughest times to be gay. As I've mentioned, I've helped numerous anonymous teenagers who have asked for help online, and some of their stories turn my stomach. I've heard of parents who threaten to disown their children or who throw them onto the street for coming out. I've even interviewed a teen whose wealthy parents influenced a judge to have him, a completely well-adjusted and mentally competent young man, put in a mental institution until he "admitted" he wasn't gay. He finally did so and now lives with his boyfriend (posing as a roommate) on his college campus in absolute fear of his powerful father finding out.

One side effect of being closeted during this period is a potential delay in the development of relationship maturity. By the time most gays graduate high school, our straight peers have already had several girlfriends, been through breakups, cheating, falling in and out of love, and learning the difference between infatuation and love. For many, the closet means that we've still not been in a serious, mutual relationship at that point. This has far-reaching implications for many adolescents. If we come out after graduation, we're entering college with the relationship maturity of a high school freshman.

As a parent, you can help to prevent this. By giving your child as much space and privacy as they require while constantly letting them know that you love them no matter what, you create a safe space for them to come out at home before they come out at school. You create a safe place for your teen to come home with their boyfriend or girlfriend who is likely also closeted. You also make it OK for her to talk to you about relationship challenges, and you can share your experiences to help her.

It's also helpful if your child sees you be critical of those who dislike or judge gay people. If you happen to be watching the news together and a politician says something anti-gay, make a comment about how offensive that is. If you have homophobic relatives, make sure they know that that kind of talk is not OK with you. This will have the effect of letting your son or daughter know that you're a safe place to come with serious issues—and there will likely be serious issues no matter how your child scores on the Kinsey scale.

Young Adulthood

After eighteen, things can still be challenging for closeted gay people, but this greatly depends on where you live in the world. Family pressure to start dating the opposite sex increases, and the absence of that dating is getting harder and harder to explain. The pressure can be so great that some gays cave in and start dating the opposite gender—even get married and have children—just to throw friends and family off the scent. Gay people who partner with the opposite gender refer to these partners as "beards." It is an umbrella term for the person they are using to throw society off the trail to discovering their homosexuality. There is nothing great about the outcome for all involved unless the straight person is a willing part of the deception—and they often are not.

Support during this phase looks similar to support during the adolescent stage except your son or daughter may be living elsewhere—a college dorm or their own apartment. This is the age when your children may start getting into more serious, long-term relationships. The kind where they bring their boy/girlfriends to meet you. It's important to be supportive of your child during the times you all spend together that may be more holiday-centric. Take the time to get to know her girlfriend as a human being. See his boyfriend as a potential son-in-law.

Be aware that if you make them choose between you and their lover, they will almost always choose their lover—as would you if your parents forbid you from dating someone you loved. So, set the homosexual issue aside for the sake of peace and enjoy the other human being they're bringing back to the family. Harmony and disharmony are both choices that all involved can make. My mom really grew attached to my partner. She thought of him like a son and told him so regularly. He lost his mother when he was sixteen, so I know how important it was for him to hear this from her.

Adulthood

If homosexuals remain closeted into their adult years, they can become quite despondent. Sadly, some become increasingly homophobic and take more desperate actions to distance themselves from suspicion, such as fighting against gay rights through joining anti-gay political movements, getting married to the opposite gender, and even having children. There is a long list of conservative congressmen and religious leaders who've been caught in gay bars or picking up gay men online.

Being gay and pretending you're straight is like holding a beach ball under water. Eventually it pops up. I know a gay man who had four children with a woman before finally admitting that he was gay and filing for divorce. The more unacceptable it is to be gay in a given social community, the more instances we see of this kind of behavior. It hurts everyone involved, including the gay man who now has to break up a family, break a woman's heart, and start over in a completely new world.

If closeted older gay people honor their true feelings at all and begin to settle down with someone of the same gender, they often move far away from home and become distant to unaccepting family. They may come home for holidays but might be leaving the love of their life at home to keep up the charade. This puts immense pressure on their relationships as partners left behind feel rejected. Anger can build over the reluctance of one of the partners to acknowledge the relationship to his family. For some, this results in an ultimatum where everyone loses.

Support for your adult gay child means having an adult conversation with them. If there are words you'd like to apologize for, do that. Tell them you love them and want them in your life, and that you need their support and patience to get through the issues you're having about their homosexuality. Tell them you're reading this book!

Siblings and Extended Family

There are many coming out stories that begin with "I told my sister first." If you think that your gay child's siblings are mature enough to handle this situation well, encourage them to also give the same supportive messages that you're giving. Tell your other child(ren) that your primary concern is the safety of all of them, including their potentially gay brother/sister. Don't be hurt if your child decides to tell her sister before she tells you. It's called a coming out *process* for a reason, and this is a very common way for a child to test out the familial waters. Another relative can be helpful here too—an aunt, uncle, grandparent, or cousin.

The important thing is that if your child asks this relative to keep the matter a secret from you, they should honor that promise unless there is concern for suicide or abuse. Breaking that trust might only further the "everyone is against me" feeling your child may have. If you're truly going to react well, those relatives can encourage your child to tell you, but it's still his or her decision.

You Are Only in Control of You

The relationship between your child and you will be constantly changing from the moment they're born. You have some very important work to do during the crucial first eighteen years to set the stage for the rest of your lives together. That work is to help your son or daughter be comfortable in their own skin. To convince them that your home is a safe place for them and to support them when outsiders bully, threaten, or hurt them.

LGBT teen suicide is mainly caused by a complete loss of hope and a feeling that there is no one to turn to. Youth who come from highly rejecting families are 8.4 times as likely to have attempted suicide as LGBT peers who report no or low levels of family rejection.[46] Make sure your home remains an open door when others seem to be closing around them.

I hope that by now I've convinced you that you are in control of your own fears, judgments, and behaviors. You can use this control to create a bridge between you and your child or you can choose to drive a wedge between yourself and the amazing,

---

[46] "Facts about Suicide," The Trevor Project, accessed December 30, 2018, http://www.thetrevorproject.org/pages/facts-about-suicide.

diverse human being you helped to bring into this world. Your resistance to create that bridge will not result in them being straight. It will only leave the two of you on opposite shores. Be courageous and choose connection.

Chapter 9: When Your Child Is Bullied

"Bullying is killing our kids. Being different is killing our kids, and the kids who are bullying are dying inside. We have to save our kids, whether they are bullied or they are bullying. They are all in pain."

— Cat Cora

In 2010, Dan Savage, a syndicated columnist and author, created a YouTube video with his partner, Terry Miller. The video was a direct response to the number of students taking their own lives after being bullied in school. It was entitled "It gets better." Since then, the It Gets Better Project™ has become a worldwide movement. More than fifty thousand videos have been viewed more than fifty million times.[47]

The project has undoubtedly saved lives, but the fact that such a project is needed is frightening and should wake us up to the reality of bullying in our schools. According to the Trevor Project, an LGBT suicide prevention program:[48]

- Suicide is the leading cause of death among young people ages ten to twenty-four.
- LGB youth are four times more likely, and questioning youth are three times more likely, to attempt suicide as their straight peers.
- Suicide attempts by LGB youth and questioning youth are four to six times more likely to result in injury, poisoning, or overdose that requires treatment from a doctor or nurse, compared to their straight peers.
- Nearly 50 percent of young transgender people have seriously thought about taking their lives, and one quarter report having made a suicide attempt.
- One out of six high school students nationwide seriously considered suicide in the past year.
- Suicide attempts are nearly two times higher among black and Hispanic youth than white youth.
- Each episode of LGBT victimization, such as physical or verbal harassment or abuse, increases the likelihood of self-harming behavior by 2.5 times on average.

[47] "What Is the It Gets Better Project?" It Gets Better Project, accessed December 30, 2018, http://www.itgetsbetter.org/pages/about-it-gets-better-project/.

[48] "Facts about Suicide," The Trevor Project, accessed December 21, 2018, http://www.thetrevorproject.org/pages/facts-about-suicide.

A Rite of Passage?

It may be tempting to think that bullying is just a rite of passage for being a kid and that everyone is bullied now and then. You may have said or thought things like:

- "What doesn't kill us makes us stronger."
- "Maybe it'll toughen him up a little to get picked on."
- "It builds character."
- "I got picked on when I was a kid, and I turned out OK."

These are risky ways to dismiss a potentially serious situation. In fact, these kinds of comments can actually make the situation worse for your child because they add your negative judgment about them being "weak" on top of the negative judgment from their peers. Make no mistake, if your child is being bullied at school, you should consider this a very serious situation and take action immediately.

The reach of technology and social media has made bullies more pervasive than ever before. Today's bullies can do their bullying anonymously, faster, and more effectively than when you were a kid. The technology can render your child powerless to stop its spread and reach them no matter where they are. Even if you physically relocate your family to get away from it, the Internet closes the gap instantly. So we aren't talking about simply name-calling from the old days. This is serious stuff. Photos and videos can be shared instantly and spread to thousands of people in minutes. Even involving the bully's parents may not be enough. Sometimes the bully's parents actually defend their child's bullying using some of the same misguided thoughts as above.

In October 2006, thirteen-year-old Megan Meier received an instant message from a boy she'd never met in person but had developed an online friendship with that said, "Everybody in O'Fallon knows who you are. You are a bad person, and everybody hates you. Have a shitty rest of your life. The world would be a better place without you." Twenty minutes later, Megan hung herself in her closet. The boy in this case was actually the mother of a former friend of Megan's posing as a fictional sixteen-year-old named Josh Evans.[49] Aside from the obviously poor judgment of that parent, it's clear that when Megan's world closed around her, she reached a level of despair that caused her to take her own life.

Let's agree to stop thinking of bullying as a rite of passage through childhood—especially since so many of our youth aren't making it through it.

It Gets Better

As most of us can testify, school can be a very difficult time socially, whether we're straight or gay. We should not underestimate the intense loneliness and hopelessness that can result from being a closeted gay kid. If parents are unsupportive or rejecting, it can be too much for some teens. Groups like the It Gets Better Project were created to remind kids that even though these years are hard, it does get better as we get older. But in order for that to happen, they must *actually get older.*

When a teenager is in school, social acceptance can seem like life or death because cliques and peer pressure seem to make the difference between eating alone and being asked by the popular kids to sit down at lunch. As we get older, we begin to understand that popularity isn't as important as it once was, and others begin liking us for who we are—scars and all. This is when "it gets better."

So how can we stack the odds in favor of our children making it past this tumultuous time? First and foremost, we must create an environment where it's safe for them to tell us what's going on at school and online. Importantly, however, they may feel they can't tell you they're being bullied without also telling you why. I speak from firsthand experience here. I was closeted during my high school years. My mom was very perceptive about me hating high school. I used to fake stomachaches to avoid going. She would ask me what was going on, but I knew I

---

[49] John Grohol, "The Power of Deception Online: The Megan Meier Story" Psychcentral.com, July 8, 2018, https://psychcentral.com/blog/the-power-of-deception-online/.

couldn't tell her I was being bullied because I'd need to tell her why and that would mean coming to terms with my own sexuality or coming out of the closet. I wasn't ready for either.

This bullying may not be the "coming out" moment you think it will be. As a teenager, your child is more likely to know they aren't straight but not sure whether that means they're gay, bisexual, or something in between. Sometimes they want to be more certain before they tell you because they'll be afraid that if they don't completely understand it themselves, you'll attempt to tell them it's just a phase or that they aren't really having same-sex attractions.

You might be thinking, "Well, how can I help them with bullying if they won't tell me because they're not ready to come out?" The way around this dilemma is to tell them that if they're being bullied at school, *why* they're being bullied is unimportant to you. Bullying is not OK, and you will support them in every way possible if it's happening to them. You need to be prepared to call the school administrators and ask for a meeting if necessary. Follow through, take this seriously, and convince the school to take it seriously too.

If the school won't take action or dismisses the bullying with the kinds of statements I opened this chapter with, tell them you will go to the school board if action isn't taken. That action should include them contacting the parents of the bully and telling them what is going on— many parents are surprised to find out their kid is bullying someone at school and will put a stop to it right then. In the few cases where parents don't take action or dismiss the bullying, the school should take steps to keep the two kids separate if possible and under adult supervision when they can't be. Teachers should be alerted that bullying is happening and told to keep an eye out for it. In serious cases, it may be necessary to switch schools or districts, get a restraining order against the bully, or consider speaking to an attorney about the possibility of a libel or slander lawsuit.

Remember that this bullying activity can be—and likely is— happening online as well, so you and your child may need to take actions with various online services. Most provide the ability to unfriend or block certain people and have privacy controls that can limit the audience of posts made by your child. Sites like Facebook and Instagram take bullying very seriously, and your child can report bullying through the site. Just enter "bullying" in the search bar. Facebook provides this very wise guidance on the matter:[50]

- **Don't retaliate**. Most bullies are looking for a reaction, so don't give them one.
- **Don't keep it a secret**. Reach out to someone you trust, like a close friend, family member, counselor, or teacher, who can give you the help and support you need.
- **Document and save**. If someone has posted something you don't like, you can print or take a screenshot of it in case you need to share it with someone you trust later.

They also provide a link to a complete bullying guide. You can find the link in Appendix B: Recommended Resources. At the time of this writing, Instagram just announced a new way to control bullying on their site called "restrict" which promises to give more control to the victims of bullying over how bullies can post about them. Let's hope this trend continues across all social media.

Suicide doesn't have an undo button and the world needs the gifts your child is bringing, so please take bullying seriously.

If Your Child Is the Bully

If you discover that your child *is* the bully, there could be many reasons for it. In the specific context of homosexuality, bullying may be a cry for help for the bully as well. As we've discussed previously, the more uncomfortable someone is with their own homosexuality (either directly or through familial and environmental influence), the more likely they are to resort to bullying those who are perceived as being gay. The idea is that if

---

[50] "What Should I Do If I'm Being Bullied, Harassed, or Attacked by Someone on Facebook," Facebook, accessed December 30, 2018, https://www.facebook.com/help/116326365118751?sr=2&query=bullying&sid=0e0sxLBRbI3d6sdas.

he is publicly making fun of someone for being gay, he must not be gay himself. This same principle can be seen over and over in political and religious circles as politicians and religious leaders who rally against homosexuality are often the ones who are later discovered playing footsie in the men's bathroom or using a gay cruising app.

In 1996, a study was conducted that first measured participants' level of homophobia. They were then connected to a device that measured the circumference of their penis (in other words, it detected an erection). According to the abstract of the study:

> "The men were exposed to sexually explicit erotic stimuli consisting of heterosexual, male homosexual, and lesbian videotapes, and changes in penile circumference were monitored. They also completed an Aggression Questionnaire (A. H. Buss & M. Perry, 1992). Both groups exhibited increases in penile circumference to the heterosexual and female homosexual videos. Only the homophobic men showed an increase in penile erection to male homosexual stimuli. The groups did not differ in aggression. Homophobia is apparently associated with homosexual arousal that the homophobic individual is either unaware of or denies."[51]

This study was conducted on adults and, to my knowledge, has never been conducted with teenagers, but it stands to reason that this issue could exist in homophobic males as long as the sexual identity crisis itself has existed. Adolescence is not only ripe for this from a biological standpoint, it's also the time when popularity would drive the ego into denial about it. Remember, anger is one expression of fear.

If your child is bullying another child for being gay, you may want to examine the environment he is in. What might make that environment conducive to hating gay people? Are there homophobic adults in his life? Is homosexuality seen as sinful in his church or among his friends? What feeds the hatred? If he is gay himself, this type of environment can ultimately foster

---

[51] Henry E. Adams, Lester W. Wright, Jr., and Bethany A. Lohr, "Is Homophobia Associated with Homosexual Arousal?" *Journal of Abnormal Psychology* 105, no. 3 (August 1996), http://doi.org/10.1037/0021-843X.105.3.440.

internalized homophobia, a subject we'll cover in Chapter 10: Internalized Homophobia. In addition to stopping the bullying immediately, you may want to follow the advice in previous chapters about creating a supportive environment for your child to come out or discuss these thoughts with you.

In Part Three, I'm hopeful that I've shown you how you can accept and support others who are gay, whether they be your child, niece, grandchild, friend, or sibling. In Part Four, I'm going to be speaking directly to gay readers, but come along for the ride. There's something for everyone there.

Part Four: Accepting Yourself

"If you begin to understand what you are without trying to change it, then what you are undergoes a transformation."

— Jiddu Krishnamurti

Chapter 10: Internalized Homophobia

"If you had a person in your life treating you the way you treat yourself, you would have gotten rid of them a long time ago."

— Cheri Huber

Imagine you live in a world where having blue eyes is considered wrong—a biblical sin, a physical disorder, a deviance from what is "normal." Everyone in your school, your church, and your family is constantly railing against blue-eyed people. Lawmakers go on TV saying that blue-eyed people will bring about the end of the world. Natural disasters are blamed on them. Protestors picket funerals of blue-eyed people. Religious leaders give sermons about the sin of being a blue-eyed person. They say that God will reject them. The news is filled with blue hate crime. There's even a deadly disease that is rumored to be spread by blue-eyed people.

In this imaginary world, all babies appear to have brown eyes. It isn't until adolescence that their true color really begins to reveal itself. For a small percentage of the population, that true color is blue, and it's clear you are going to be one of them. You quickly purchase colored contacts before anyone notices.

Now that you're under the radar, consciously or unconsciously, you'll likely select some form of one of these two options:

1. Accept that being blue-eyed is a normal part of who you are and that you're entitled to be treated equally, even if you may be the only person who believes that.
2. Agree with the world you're surrounded by and begin hating your blue eyes and yourself. Become fearful of your blue eyes and the rejection you'll encounter in every facet of your life. Resent other blue-eyed people who won't wear their contacts and work to enact laws against blue-eyed people.

While this fictional world is a bit contrived in some sense, the experience of a gay teen is similar to the one experienced in that hypothetical world. There are still large parts of the United States and many parts of the world where homophobia is prevalent and, in some cases, being discovered as gay can be a death sentence. If you add in conservative politics and sprinkle in some religion, you can end up with entire communities that treat homosexuality as a defect and a sin. It even permeates the one place a child is supposed to feel safe—home.

What Is Internalized Homophobia?

Internalized homophobia is the second choice above. It's also called "heterosexism," "self-prejudice," "homonegativity," and "self-directed homophobia." How do you know you're going down this path? Here are a few telltale signs: [52]

- If you have a partner, you force them to stay in the closet with you or play a role of "friend" when in public
- You feel contempt or disgust towards LGBT people who don't "blend in"
- You can't come out, even in safe communities and settings
- You've tried to change your sexual orientation through conversion therapy, prayer, or medical treatment
- You cannot have emotionally intimate or romantic relationships, even though you desire it
- You think about committing suicide because of the way *you* feel about *your* sexuality (not necessarily because of the way *others* feel about it or treat you)

When you choose this path, you act as a channel for all the fear and hate that surround you. To quote the Emperor in *Star Wars: Return of the Jedi*, you "let the hate flow through you." Here are some additional things to watch out for:[52]

- Denial, ranging from aggressive and hateful behavior to denying yourself the life and love you desire
- Lying to yourself about attraction and sexuality
- Feeling disgust towards other LGBT people who don't express themselves in a heteronormative way
- Anger and resentment toward other LGBT people for being out or proud of their identity
- Transphobia, gender policing, shaming, or harming LGBT individuals who do not fit into the gender binary
- Anger or embarrassment that other LGBT people "represent" you

---

[52] "Internalized Homophobia," Revel & Riot, accessed December 30, 2018, http://www.revelandriot.com/resources/internalized-homophobia/.

- Mental or physical health issues with no known underlying cause
- Inability to have intimacy, emotionally or physically
- Low self-esteem/negative self-view that can lead to avoiding substantial relationships or others avoiding you
- Dishonesty, which can prevent or destroy trust between friends and family
- Verbal or physical abuse within friendships and romantic relationships
- Deep shame about sexual experiences
- Ambivalence, loneliness, or isolation
- Inability to have emotionally intimate sexual encounters
- Preventing yourself from having sex even if you desire it

I suffered from internalized homophobia during adolescence and even into early adulthood. At one point, I remember working with gay author and therapist Joe Kort and telling him that I resented the more flamboyant people in the gay pride parade and wished they'd make more of an effort to fit in. He said it sounded like I had some internalized homophobia going on. I'd never heard the term and was immediately jarred. Me? Homophobic? How ridiculous. I'm an out, gay male! But he was right.

I've done a lot of work around this personally, with professional help and on my own, to understand how my version of "normal" was so influenced by my local surroundings and suburban social circles. It had never occurred to me that I'd succumbed to a definition of normality defined by those surroundings and people rather than celebrating individuality and diversity.

This had far-reaching implications for me as a gay man even after I came out. I dated only men who were "straight acting." I only had gay friends who were masculine. How many great people did I exorcise from my life through all of this? That thought stays with me today. When I feel myself being uncomfortable around someone these days (it's rare, but it happens), I remind myself of how brave these people are to embrace who they are so fully and how my discomfort is really my old thought patterns of "normal" intruding on the situation.

They say that you can't truly love another or be loved by them if you can't love yourself. Nowhere will this surface more with homosexual men and women than with internalized homophobia. Couples that include a partner with internalized homophobia are really operating at differing levels of comfort with homosexuality in general. That difference can result in constant fighting with partners over issues of individuality ("Do you have to be so flamboyant/butch around my parents?"). And that's assuming a relationship can even be started. To someone with internalized homophobia, other gay people will often be seen as inadequate or missing the mark. Too feminine, too butch, too touchy-feely, too emotional, too into gay rights, too open about their sexuality, too _____. Fill in the blank with the excuse of the day for remaining outside of a relationship of any kind with another person of the same gender while still being attracted to them.

Accepting Your Body

I am what's known in the gay community as a "bear," which, as you might imagine, means I have a larger frame with a hairy body. I won't bore you with all the body type descriptions in the gay community because there are many and some of the granularity can be a bit ridiculous, especially to the straight community. There is another type to know that is necessary for my point though, and that's called a "twink." Opinions differ in the gay community, but the least controversial definition of a twink is a guy with a swimmer's build and a usually smooth body. As a practical matter, most bears are attracted to other bears, and most twinks are attracted to other twinks. There is a small subset of each type that likes the other, however. Non-bears (including twinks) that like bears call themselves "chasers." I happen to fall into that subset of bears that is primarily attracted to chasers.

Why am I telling you this? Because being part of this subset of bears has taught me some tough lessons about self-acceptance. My attraction to guys who have an entirely different build than me—and my non-attraction to those with the same build—made me harshly view my own body in the mirror for quite a few years. This is an experience unique to gay people from the best that I can determine. Straight men aren't looking in the mirror thinking they need to grow bigger breasts so they can look like the big-breasted women they like. Gay men and women, on the other hand, actually are attracted to their same gender. If the body you are attracted to happens to look like your own, thumbs up. But if it differs in uncontrollable ways, like it does in my case, it takes quite an effort not to go on crash diets trying to get a slender body and shave my body hair trying to be the chaser I'm attracted to. This is more than just me trying to deceive a potential mate or portray more of what they want. It's about my own acceptance of my looks, period.

The same experience happens on the other side of the subset, by the way. Chasers are constantly trying to look more like bears by growing facial hair, putting on weight, etc. What both sides are missing is, if a bear wants a bear, there are plenty to choose from, and the same applies to chasers. So why not embrace your "bearness," or your "non-bearness," or whatever in between you were given, and let others find you attractive for who you are. This doesn't mean you shouldn't exercise or be healthy if that inspires you, but if you've got a big frame, love it, be it fully. Others will be attracted to your confidence, and there *is* someone you will find attractive who will love you just the way you are.

One of the tougher lessons I learned about this was in my early thirties. I was in a very toxic relationship with a younger guy who was likely not attracted to guys like me and who was arguably bisexual. He and I created a relationship that was codependent and destructive to both of us. He wanted financial security and support and a mentor, and I wanted to be his mentor and was very attracted to him. Once we began being sexual together, he began to use my insecurity around finding another guy like him as leverage to keep me in his life, and I used my money and financial security to keep him in mine.

I haven't seen him for many years, but I imagine that neither of us is too proud of our behavior in that relationship. He used to say things like, "You'll never find a guy like me who will find you attractive." For a long time, I believed him because *I* didn't find *myself* attractive. When we finally broke up, I discovered the chaser community and met my current partner. He and I have been together for over fifteen years as I write this. In fact, my (now) husband, Jesse, is really the one who taught me to embrace my "bearness," and I'm forever grateful for it.

A Note About Being Transgender

The section above is not meant to be a lecture about accepting your *gender* if you don't feel like that gender on the inside. I readily acknowledge that this book doesn't spend an adequate amount of attention to the specific struggles of those who are struggling with gender issues. This was a conscious decision on my part because, while gender plays a role in sexual orientation, it serves neither homosexuality nor gender identity to conflate the two or make them seem necessarily connected. For example, the sex you were assigned at birth may be male, but your internal sense of gender identity may be female. If you were to decide to go through the process to change your body to a female, you will still be attracted to men and you would typically identify as a straight woman at that point. Because gender identity and sexual orientation are separate, I decided to focus on the homosexual issue only. See Appendix B: Recommended Resources for specific recommendations around gender identity issues.

My aim with this section was to help you see self-hatred behavior if you have it, but it's beyond the scope of this (or any) book to get you past it. If you are gay and are surrounded by hate towards homosexuality, it may take a strong will to resist it, but the other option is to hate a core part of who you are. If you identify with any of what you've read, it's important that you consider seeing a professional therapist who can help you through it. Your future self will thank you.

Chapter 11: If You're Being Bullied

"When people see you're happy doing what you're doing, it sort of takes the power away from them to tease you about it."

— Wendy Mass

"People who love themselves don't hurt other people. The more we hate ourselves, the more we want others to suffer."

— Dan Pearce

I was bullied through much of my non-adult life. I had a pretty solid case of Asshole Proximity Disorder, never seeming to be far enough from one to be spared from their teasing. In elementary school and junior high, it was because of my weight. In high school, homosexuality and the first signs of baldness were added into the mix. While I know some teens today have it way worse than I did—I was spared from cyberbullying, for example—I do know a thing or two about being bullied and about those who do the bullying. In this chapter, we're going to get into what makes bullies tick, how you can fight back, and how you can gain a perspective that might just make the bullying seem less important—which may even have the side effect of making it go away altogether.

Personal Security

Throughout this chapter, you're going to see me mention the ideas of security and insecurity, so it's appropriate to spend a bit of time explaining what I mean by those terms.

Security is a complex psychological topic, but in essence it boils down to this: being comfortable in your own skin. This will be very difficult to achieve if you're suffering from internalized homophobia (see Chapter 10: Internalized Homophobia) because by definition you're not comfortable in your own skin if you are negatively judging a core part of who you are. Being secure means that you are very difficult to knock off your horse.

I struggled for many years to really feel secure. It really solidified for me in my thirties. Around this time, I went back to college in a second or third attempt at getting my degree (I'm losing track). As a thirty-something, I found myself in classes with much younger people, some just out of high school. One semester, I took a computer programming class, and, because I'd worked around computers my whole career, I found the class to be very easy. So, when it came time to choose lab partners, two of the younger students jumped to my side. I'm sure it was because they were hoping it would increase their grades and not just because I'm stupendously attractive.

One cold winter day, I walked into class wearing some designer Isotoner gloves. My class partners and I had developed a bit of a fun relationship, so they were comfortable with me, and one of them teased me for the gloves. He said in a mocking, lispy, and feminine tone, "Awwww. Are your hands cold? Those are *ssspecial* gloves you have on." I'll never forget what I said back to him because it turned out to be a turning point in my understanding of security and all the bullying I'd been through in my life. I said, "Look, I know at this stage of your life this kind of thing is important to you, but one day, when you've gotten some more distance between you and high school, you'll realize how little you give a shit about other people's opinions of you or your clothing."

A light bulb went off for me. *That's* security! Not giving a crap what other people think about me. Dressing for my own comfort and style. Being who I chose to be instead of who everyone else wanted me to be so *they* were comfortable. We're all on a journey in life. Part of these boys' journey was getting over what made them uncomfortable; part of mine was creating a little of that discomfort for them. "Mission accomplished. You're welcome," I thought with a smile. If only I'd gotten this sooner!

With this chapter, I'll attempt to help you understand security so you can set your own sail for it and reach the destination much faster than I did. You might be thinking, "Security? I'm getting picked on here, and that's all you've got to offer me?" Well, no, but if it was, it would be all you need. OK, I realize that telling you *what* security is doesn't quite tell you *how* to get it, and I admit that the journey was long for me, but it doesn't have to be. We're getting there. Patience, grasshopper.

A WORD OF CAUTION: I do want to take a moment to make a distinction between verbal teasing and physical abuse. As the saying goes, sticks and stones may break my bones, but words will never hurt me. We'll work on what you can do to handle the words part, but broken bones are not OK, and being threatened with physical violence is serious business. You should definitely enlist help when your physical well-being is threatened or if the name-calling is impacting you in a way that's reinforcing internalized homophobia or is causing depression, an inability to concentrate, falling grades, or mental and/or physical health issues. I'll provide some guidance on how to do that in this chapter as well. Buckle up!

Tactics and Strategies

When I was in junior high, I was teased pretty frequently about my weight. My mom, I think believing that there might be some issues from her divorcing my dad, set me up with a counselor to talk. When I told him about the teasing, he gave me a great tip. He said, "The next time someone teases you about your weight, just tell them, 'Yeah, you're right. I could stand to lose a few pounds.'" Could it really be that easy? The next week I was given a chance to try it out, and when I did, my bully just stammered, his voice trailing off as he said, "Yeah," and then he walked away.

I realized at that moment that what fueled him—what made his day—was my defensive reaction. No matter how witty a response I came up with (and I was pretty witty), it was like fuel for his asshole machine. As soon as I agreed with him, his incentive to keep repeating it was gone. He never teased me again. This doesn't mean I took his criticism to heart, however. In this case, it was true that I was a bit overweight. The way I put it wasn't being self-critical, just honest about what I already knew. I didn't say, "Yeah I'm a real fatty, aren't I?" My agreement was the kinder, gentler version.

But what if you're being teased for something that *isn't* true or that you're not currently prepared to admit to? When I was bullied for being gay, the rumor mill was in full force. This was *big news* at my high school, and the word spread quickly that I'd made a move on a rather popular (and handsome, I might add) guy over the previous weekend. This was true, and that handsome guy participated in every bit of it all the way to the end (I had the proverbial Monica Lewinski dress back at home to prove it) but, of course, he left all that out when he told everyone about it. Whether he intended to or not, he put me in a place where I could only admit that I was gay to spill the beans on his part of the event or deny that I was gay and that any of it happened, thereby protecting him. Devious.

I was pretty taken aback by the whole thing. I was definitely not expecting him to tell anyone about what we did. Some money went missing from my mom's bathroom the night he was there and that might have had something to do with him wanting to end the friendship, but I digress. In a panic, I denied everything. I tried to play it off like it didn't bother me, but the more that people moved away from me at lunch, the more it became clear that it did bother me. This only fueled some of the assholes. If one of them passed me in between classes, they'd pretend to be friendly and say, "Hey, Sean! What's up?" Surprised that anyone was talking to me, I'd say, "Uh, hey, not much," and then they'd say, "So, have you sucked anyone's dick lately?" and then they'd laugh and walk off, leaving me on the verge of tears and full of anger.

This wasn't a time for me to pull my earlier tactic from junior high. "Oh yes, I have! My own, just this morning. I probably should cut back." It wouldn't have worked out like the weight loss one. In that case, my self-deprecation was based on a little obvious truth: that I actually could stand to lose a few pounds. In this case, it would have sounded like sarcasm, which would have only fueled the asshole machine. Believe me, I had a ton of sarcasm on the ready. "Yes, I have. I'd suck yours, but small bones are dangerous." "Why do you ask? Your girlfriend not giving you any? Oh, you don't have a girlfriend, do you?" None of these would have worked and in some cases would have made the situation much worse, but they did make me laugh on the inside, which helped lighten up an otherwise crappy situation.

Unfortunately, when you're being teased about something you aren't even comfortable enough to accept about yourself—as was the case in my situation above—things get a bit more complicated. My insecurity was the thing that gave them all the power. Not only because it fueled their incentive to keep jabbing me but also because it prevented me from just saying, "Yeah, I'm gay. Big deal." So, in retrospect, that might have been a good time for me to come out and deal with the fallout from that, if there was to be any. After all, I was dealing with fallout anyway; at least I could have turned on my "don't give a shit what you think" switch and meant it.

Note: Before you decide that coming out is the right step for you, you should definitely read Chapter 12: Coming Out because there are some very important considerations before you do.

Allies May Appear

Chances are, if you're being bullied, so are others. It's rare that a bully is a nice guy to everyone but you. This could mean that you might start to build allegiances with others who share the same disdain for the same person/people. The more people that band together, the safer things get, and the more likely the bully will be stopped. So be on the lookout for other victims of this bully and reach out if possible.

In my case, I had some friends who stuck through the whole ordeal with me. They probably were tolerating some bullying of their own that they never told me about. My social situation at school definitely changed to me being less popular, but that didn't mean there weren't still people on my side. Look for those people in your life, let them know how much you appreciate them, and focus your time and energy on them rather than the bully.

It's About Them, Not About You

If there's one thing I'm 100% certain of, bullying is always about the bully, *not* about you. Keep that in mind. In the case of being teased for being gay, studies show that there is a high probability that your homophobic bully is gay himself and suffering from a bad case of internalized homophobia. Perhaps you are a bit flamboyant and secure about being gay, and he's envious because he's too scared of his homosexual urges to act on them. He will lash out at you for being who he wishes he could be but feels that he can't. That frustration comes across as anger and bullying. You can't ever own his problem, but it's helpful to know that no matter what he says to you, it's really more about him. Treat his words like Teflon and try to feel a little pity for him instead of anger.

If the antidote for bullying is security, it's clear that bullies are very insecure. Anytime someone needs to tease or put someone else down to feel better, they are putting up their insecurity in neon lights for the world to see. Look at me! I'm insecure about the size of my penis, so I'm going to tease you about not being manly enough. Look at me! I'm insecure about my family life, so I'm going to create social instability for you. Look at me! I'm insecure about my looks, so I'm going to make fun of you for yours! And on and on. I'm not trying to create sympathy for bullies, but it really is a cry for help for many of them. That's not your job as the one being bullied; just be aware of it because it puts a context around the bullying that might soften the blow a bit.

My last two years of high school were slightly improved by the fact that I joined the Drama Club. At my school, that particular group had a few other misfits and we all bonded nicely. I ended up getting cast as the lead bad guy in a couple of plays for the school. After my bullies watched me act on stage, it seemed to make them respect me more because the bullying almost came to a complete stop. Your mileage may vary here but do look for Gay/Straight Alliances at your school or join a club or sport where you can fit in and don't be afraid to bail on them if you don't.

It Gets Better

By now, you've probably seen lots of YouTube videos from the It Gets Better Project™. If you haven't, go watch some of them and then come back. I'll wait. [Sean disappears to play video games for a while.] Back? Good. Nice, right? You may be dismissively thinking, "Sure, it gets better." That reveals a challenge with the It Gets Better Project. It sounds too . . . trite? Too good to be true, and you're probably sitting in a big pile of doo doo right now, and there may seem to be no sign of an escape route. That's the kind of thinking that leads to suicidal thoughts, so let's address that first.

When I hear about another teen suicide, I get so frustrated and sad. I wish I could back up time, grab that teen by the shoulders, look them square in the eye and say, "YOU MATTER, GODDAMNIT! The world is waiting for your gifts, and these clowns who are teasing you are all going to be off to college or working at fast food in a year or two. None of this will matter then. But your absence will leave a hole in the world from all the people who will mourn the loss of you and those who will never get a chance to meet you, be influenced by you, or be loved by you over the next eighty years. If people have disowned you, wipe your feet and move on. There's love to be had and a world is waiting to show you, but none of that will matter if you do this because there's no undo button for suicide."

Sorry. I'm getting a little worked up just typing that. I'll have more to say about this in Chapter 13: A Life Worth Living, but suffice to say that, yes, life does get better than the way you're experiencing it during adolescence, so the people in the videos are telling the truth. One day you'll have your own Isotoner gloves moment. If you don't know what that means, I just caught you skipping around the book.

You might be asking, "Why does it get better?" Well, for one thing, High School Survival 101 is around navigating intense social cliques and fickle popularity contests. One minute you're on top, the next the bottom. All because someone that used to be at the bottom tossed a juicy rumor onto social media. Maybe you did or said something stupid (otherwise known as being human), but your fellow students at Hunger Games High decided it was time for you to pay for it with your popularity—the only currency more valuable than grades.

The further you get away from high school, the further you get away from this social BS. The good news is there is literally no time in your life after high school where you will be crammed into a confined piece of land with so much immaturity and social pressure. Much of that pressure vanishes instantly the very day you graduate. In the months leading up to that day, many of your classmates will have been taking the SATs and applying for colleges all over the country. Some will join the military. What's certain is that cliques will dissolve almost immediately. High school is a mash-up of people who share your zip code and usually don't want to be there. College is open to all zip codes and is voluntary, so, in theory, lots of people from all over come together by choice.

There's a twist with college. In high school, your teachers hounded you for your grades, homework, reading assignments, attendance in class, etc. In college, your instructors will put much of that responsibility on you. After all, it's your money. If you want to waste it getting all D's or F's, that's your business. This added responsibility makes most students feel more like adults and less like kids. There's a sense of "We need to wear our big boy and girl pants now." Suddenly those social cliques and the teasing seem so . . . well . . . old school. When I say suddenly, I'm not kidding. This transition can happen *very* quickly. So stick around for it. Even if you're not going to college, many of your classmates are, and the social circles will greatly shift. Your bully's opportunities to tease you will vanish and so will his/her audience.

This might be a good time to mention that it was during this period, right before high school graduation, when my nemesis and I made up (no kissing, unfortunately—did I mention how cute he was?). I wouldn't say we were the best of friends, but we could be in the same room and talk to each other. I even helped him with his homework a little bit. What made the change possible? Likely the knowledge that our social lives were about to dissolve and reform differently. Looking back, I can tell you that they definitely did.

When It's Time for Help

It's often a good idea to get some adult advice no matter how minor the bullying seems to you, but there are some times when you absolutely *must* reach out for help:
- Threats of or actual physical violence to you or others

- Stalking behavior or harassment
- Threats of extortion or blackmail
- Threats that extend out of school into your workplace or extracurricular activities
- When adults join in on the bullying. This includes adults who look the other way while it's occurring (unfortunately, it happens).
- When your ability to concentrate on your schoolwork is affected and/or your grades become affected
- When you start inventing reasons not to go to school
- You start to believe your bully or take over for him/her when they're not around
- If you begin to feel depressed, hopeless, or suicidal
- If social media or cyberbullying is involved

If any of the above behavior is coming from family members, getting help may be trickier but not impossible. There are groups to turn to. The Trevor Project (thetrevorproject.org) offers texting and chat options as well as live operators who can help you. Some schools have gay-straight alliances you can join as well. One thing is worth repeating: if you're suffering from internalized homophobia, these kinds of groups might only serve to reinforce your homophobia because you may meet people there who reinforce your stereotypes or who represent the kind of thinking you're not comfortable with in yourself. If you have some of these thought patterns, it's best to start with a therapist. Overcoming internalized homophobia often requires some professional assistance. It's worth it. Fight for your right to lead a fulfilling life free of judgment—especially if that judgment is coming from you.

When You Witness Bullying

If you are a witness to bullying and you do nothing, you are joining in with the bullies. This is especially true if violence is involved, but even verbal abuse that goes unchallenged is tacit approval for the bully that their behavior is OK. This is especially true if you are an adult witnessing the bullying of children and do nothing. Your lack of action is seen as a green light for the bully and those considering joining in that this is acceptable behavior.

Unfortunately, there are teachers who willingly turn away when gay children are bullied or even join in because of their own religious convictions around homosexuality. If you are such a teacher or administrator and you feel defensive about that behavior, this paragraph is for you: Quit. You are not in the right line of work if you see your job as preaching morality at school or somehow judging the human beings that are developing under your care. If you join in with other children who are bullying, you are applying your adult authority to the judgment of a much younger bully who probably has his or her own issues with homosexuality.

If you're a fellow student, use your own judgment to decide whether to risk your own safety by speaking up or stepping in. At minimum you should call an adult over immediately. Try to get as many allies involved as you can because there is power in numbers, and those numbers can make the difference between life and death for the victim of bullying.

We've spent a lot of time talking about bullying in this book because it's such a serious issue with long-lasting ramifications if it's not handled properly by both the victim and those witnessing it or supporting the victim. I'll reiterate again here that if you're being bullied, get help. The time and place you're in seems like your whole world when it's actually such a small portion of the world you live in. Not only will you be able to move far away from such people soon enough, you'll also see what a small part of your life that school is. Bullying tries to close the world around you. If it helps, imagine that one day that bully will be the one washing your Mercedes.

Chapter 12: Coming Out

"My only regret about being gay is that I repressed it for so long. I surrendered my youth to the people I feared when I could have been out there loving someone. Don't make that mistake yourself. Life's too damn short."

— Armistead Maupin

Coming out of the closet probably seems like one of the biggest decisions you'll ever make, and it is big in the sense that your life will take a truer path moving forward, and you'll likely see the day you came out as a decisive day where you took off your mask and presented your true self to the world. Your authenticity will attract people to you, but it can repel others, so you need to be prepared for that. In this chapter, we're going to discuss the considerations to coming out.

Before we get there, it's important to clarify what I mean by "coming out." When I use this term, I mean telling others about whatever your sexual orientation is. That is a process insomuch as you probably aren't going to tell everyone all at once. You're going to tell the most trusted person first and continue to go down the line. Eventually you will "be out." Some use the term "coming out" to describe the process of *figuring out* their orientation. When I refer to "coming out," I mean the process of telling others about the orientation you've already accepted about yourself.

Location, Location, Location

"Start where you are. Use what you have. Do what you can."

— Arthur Ashe

Where you live plays probably the most important role in deciding whether to come out or not. The reason for this is that human beings are tribal in nature, even in today's connected world. Those who are born or move into your community are pressured to conform to norms for your neighborhood, city, state, and even country in some cases. That pressure and the resulting rejection and acceptance of behavioral norms create a culture unique to your geographic area.

The United States, where I live, presents its own geographic spectrum of acceptance, but I must consider that some of you may be in countries that are openly hostile to homosexuality. As I write this, terrorists are throwing gay men from rooftops and gay people are being stoned to death in some

African and Arab nations. This is serious business. If this describes the situation in your locale, do *not* come out until you are safely in a location that accepts homosexuality culturally. That might mean anything from moving to the next city to seeking asylum in another country, but take this as your first consideration to coming out.

There are small towns all across America where everyone knows your name—and your business. Where the teacher who teaches you in school or the preacher who preaches to you in church is the same one who taught or preached to your parents or older siblings. Where the biggest employer in town may be the same place your family has worked for generations. This environment, especially if it has tight-knit religious influences, can be very challenging to come out in. It's especially difficult to come out gradually in places like this because the news that you're gay will spread like fire on gasoline. You may also be finding that locating a mate is rather difficult because even if there are other closeted gays in your town and you find each other, you risk being the talk of the town. Don't despair, and definitely don't feel trapped. It may seem difficult to imagine getting out of that area and situation, but it will become more and more likely if you focus on that as your top priority.

You may be a strong, independent thinker and be saying to yourself, "Screw 'em. I am who I am, and they can just deal with it." If you live in a small town like this, I strongly advise you not to underestimate the amount of trouble a town full of people can bring to your doorstep—sometimes literally. Your safety and security need to rise above your ability to be openly authentic in your town. That being said, it should probably be your number one goal in life to move out of that situation when you are legally and financially able to do it, so you can come out in a safe place.

Location can also mean your parents' house. If you live in a fairly accepting community but with your parents who are anything but receptive to the idea of you being gay, coming out can be *very* risky. As unfair as this sounds, until you are eighteen, you are not legally able to make some decisions and, more importantly, your parents are legally entitled to make some you may greatly dislike.

As I mentioned earlier, I once interviewed a young gay man who was the son of a very wealthy and powerful man. His father reacted so poorly to him coming out that he convinced (read: paid off) a judge to commit his son to an insane asylum. He was kept there until he "admitted" that was not gay. Once he was out of the institution, his father's financial support in college was dependent upon him keeping the secret that his roommate in college was actually his boyfriend.

There are also well-documented stories of teenagers who are literally kidnapped in the middle of the night by "pray the gay away" organizations hired by their parents. These essentially operate as concentration camps to instill religious morality into the "participants." Because they are questionably legal in the United States, these places often operate in foreign countries where the rights of the minors involved are considered even less. If you wish to see a documentary about this, watch *Kidnapped for Christ*.

Again, your safety and security are the most important things. We will discuss some ways for you to test the waters in the sections that follow, but if you think your safety or security is at risk from parents who may act aggressively against you if they knew you were gay, you should *not* come out until it is safer for you to do so.

Why Come Out?

Assuming you live in a safe location for coming out, you may be thinking, "Why come out at all? Wouldn't it be simpler if I just kept this to myself?" It would definitely be simpler, but the question is: Simpler for whom? Definitely not you. One teenager I'll call Tristan told me about the harrowing time he was having coming out slowly. With some people knowing and some people not, he was continually having to police what he said in front of certain people, and the stress of keeping track of who knew and who didn't was taking a toll on him.

Remaining in the closet is a difficult, stressful thing that gets even harder to do as you get older. More and more, your straight peers will become involved in relationships with the opposite sex. The absence of such a relationship will become harder and harder for you to cover.

In the worst outcomes of this scenario, you get a mate of the opposite sex to try to throw everyone off the trail. Some people actually get married and have children before they finally can't take it any longer and come out, dismantling their family and causing hardship for all involved.

Coming out is more about you than others. At some point, you will weigh your own discomfort against the discomfort you believe others will suffer from knowing the truth. When the discomfort of holding back who you really are or sharing who you love with the world outweighs the discomfort others may feel from that, you will come out.

I often tell people that I came out to stop homophobic people from saying ignorant things in front of me. When I was in my early thirties, a new guy had started at my work and I made a point to subtly drop a few hints to him that I was gay. Nothing too forward, I just didn't bother changing some "he's" to "she's" when I talked about my weekends. He and I became friends over a few months, and he later confessed to me that he was homophobic before he met me. Since he'd gotten to know me, he'd started to see gay people in an entirely different light. This probably wouldn't have happened if he said something homophobic as a joke early on. I would have steered clear of him, and we likely would have never become friends.

We don't often know we're in the presence of a gay person the way we do with someone of a different skin color or ethnicity. So it isn't uncommon for a gay person to hear a coworker being called a "fag" or "gay" as an insult or as teasing. I'd prefer to make the homophobic person do the policing of their language rather than have to hide who I am for their comfort or pleasure.

There is at least one other reason you may want to come out: sharing the person you love with others. If you have found a special person and you are deeply in love, you will likely find it very stifling to pretend otherwise in the presence of others, and your special someone might feel offended that you're keeping him in the closet with you. Love is meant to be shared. When I brought my first boyfriend over, it was about as nonconfrontational as I could make it. Slowly at Christmas, I began putting my hand on his shoulder or around his waist. It eventually graduated into kissing him affectionately in front of my family the way my siblings were able to do with their partners. Today, my family thinks of my partner as part of the family. My mom considered him to be a son and loved him dearly. He even put his career on hold to help me care for her while she was dying of cancer in our home. I could not have done it without him.

Our families can feel our love for each other because it's palpable. It may not work out like this for everyone, but your ability to share your love with those who will appreciate it is only possible if you come out. Again, remember that any discomfort that others feel as a result of you loving someone of the same sex is *their* journey, not yours. Don't over-own it.

Who to Come Out To

Of all the coming out decisions to make, this will be one of the hard ones. The trick here is to pick someone you've got a pretty good sense will react positively or at least neutrally, and preferably someone you think might be able to keep a secret in case you decide to put the brakes on the process. This person may or may not be family. There are a couple of generalized things about coming out that I've found to be true in many cases:

People who have not demonstrated any outward hatred of gays are likely going to react better than you fear they will. When I told my mom I was gay, she told me she was just waiting for me to tell her. I had a great deal of angst leading up to that moment that turned out to be wasted stress, and I've heard the same from other LGBT people. They braced for the worst and were pleasantly surprised with how smooth it went. You might be surprised to find out that your folks, like my mom, already suspect or even know that you're gay and are just waiting for you to tell them.

People who *have* demonstrated outward hatred of gays are likely going to react poorly—at *least* initially. People who are homophobic are operating from a place of fear (homophobia is literally the *fear* of homosexuals/homosexuality). Homophobia isn't much different than arachnophobia (fear of spiders). When we're scared, we take either a fight or flight response to whatever is the cause. In the case of spiders, probably flight. In response to homosexuality, probably fight. We will cover this more in just a bit, but it is impossible to reason with someone who is operating in a fear response. You can't tell someone who is paralyzed with fear that the spider on the wall is harmless. People with phobias use their rational minds to defend their phobia, not to counter it. They see it as a survival mechanism.

So, if you come out to a homophobic person, don't expect them to act "rationally" or be able to wow them with scientific evidence, biblical studies, or verbal assurances. They are almost literally not hearing you. It doesn't mean you can't tell them you're gay, but be prepared for a rough ride and a cooling down period. Only if they reach that period will you be able to reason with them at all. Dropping this book in their lap during the peak of their emotional reaction will likely result in it being used to start a fire in the fireplace. You also may need to be prepared for the idea that they *never* become OK with it. It could happen. When you're facing this type of person, your being gay can be a relationship ender. If that person is your parent, this will be a very difficult period for you. As I stated above, coming out is more about you than them. For you to face the risk of ending the relationship, being who you really are must be more important than making them comfortable. On the other hand, if the only way they will love you is if you hide who you really are, they aren't loving the real you anyway. They're loving the fake you. The one that keeps them from being uncomfortable. That discomfort belongs to them so, again, try not to over-own it.

No matter who you come out to first, it is *very* difficult for that person to keep that secret. This is especially true if the person you tell needs someone else's support. It's unfair to tell them something like this and then tell them they are bound to secrecy so they can't seek help for themselves around any issues *they* have with the news. Remember, when you come out of the closet, you may feel a ton better, but you've just potentially dropped a bombshell on your parents, who may need time and support from their peers or professionals to figure out *their* issues around it. For example, some parents go through a blaming themselves stage. What did they do "wrong" that "made" you gay? Groups like PFLAG will help with this, but you should be sensitive to the fact that you just saying, "Hey, Mom, I'm gay, can you please pass me the sugar?" may not be the end of the conversation for them. So be prepared for the cat to get out of the bag and start running around your entire family circle.

This is especially true for friends in school. Some topics are just too hot to hold onto, and teenagers are still learning how to earn trust and keep secrets. It is likely that coming out slowly at school will be a very difficult thing to do. Plan accordingly.

Some people feel betrayed when you tell them. No matter when you come out, there will always be a period that you didn't. Close friends and family may tell you that they're hurt that you didn't tell them sooner. You may be sitting on a stack of lies by the time you come out of the closet. That's a normal part of being in the closet, and getting away from lying may be one of the reasons you have for coming out in the first place. If someone expresses disappointment that you lied or didn't trust them enough to share this earlier, explain to them that keeping this secret has been very stressful for you and that coming out is a way to end the secrets. Tell them that that you appreciate their support now that you're ready to accept it. Remind them that this took an incredible amount of courage to share and that isn't because of them, it's because of the gravity of the issue and the importance of being sure.

Tell the person you're closest with first. When I came out, I started with my best friend. She is older than me, and I knew she would keep it to herself until I was ready. The males in my family were the last ones I told. I've spent a lot of time trying to figure out why. I'm sure it has to do with the fact that the males in my life are extremely masculine, and I assumed they believed that being gay is feminine. You need to think about your situation and let your gut guide you through the decision about who to tell.

When to Come Out

Aside from the considerations above around location that have a "when" component to them, as a general rule you should come out when being closeted is becoming harder than being out would be. For some, that bar is pretty low. For example, if you're surrounded by supportive family and friends who will love you no matter what and you live in a community that is open to homosexuality, coming out is much less risky, and the benefits of not having to lie and be secretive will far outweigh the risks to your safety.

For others, the bar is very high. Coming out could mean homelessness, incarceration, forced gay reparative therapy, physical or mental abuse, or worse. If you suspect that any of those are a possibility, your survival must take precedence over your desire to be authentic. You should immediately make it your number one goal to get to a place where you can be who you really are. That might mean waiting until you are legally able to decide your own fate, saving money, living with a distant relative, or branching out on your own at your first legal opportunity.

Whatever you do, do not make any rash decisions before you're legally not a minor. Your parents can use those actions against you in ways you will probably not like. For example, if you run away, you could be labeled a troubled youth who is uncooperative. Your parents can then take advantage of a system that may not be on your side. I strongly encourage you to get help if you're in this situation. Find a youth gay center, speak to the

Trevor Project or a trusted distant relative (if you're certain they can be trusted not to call your parents), reach out for help online in places like Reddit. There is a subreddit there called lgbteens where you will get supportive advice from other teens in your situation. If you're unfamiliar with the vast frontier that is Reddit, all you need to know is that it is an anonymous place where people gather—and like all places like this, there are great people saying intelligent, humanitarian things on some areas of the site *and* there are really terrible people saying unintelligent, unhumanitarian things on other areas that they would probably never say to anyone's face—or at all if they didn't have the cover of anonymity. But the lgbteens subreddit (reachable at https://www.reddit.com/r/LGBTeens) is a safe, moderated place where you can have real back-and-forth exchanges with other gay teens. You are almost guaranteed to find supportive, great people of all walks of life there. They've either been there or done that and will likely point you in the right direction if you're confused or uncertain what to do next. It's not therapy, it's not mentoring, but it is community when you are feeling alone and want to remain anonymous.

When to come out is a very personal and individual decision. Every gay person has their own "coming out" story. If you're surrounded by loving family and friends who you know are accepting no matter what, you can begin the conversation at any point along the journey. If your personal safety is in doubt, take it slowly and cautiously.

How to Come Out

As I've mentioned several times, coming out is not an event, it's a process. The speed of that process is in your control *to some extent*. Recall above that once you tell someone you're gay there is no guarantee that it will remain a secret, so you must at least prepare for the contingency that it will be difficult to unring that bell. To that end, it's often a good idea to bring up the topic of gays with those close to you in a nonpersonal way. For example, talk about a (perhaps fictional) kid from your or a nearby school who's gay. Keep it positive and see what reaction you get.

Something like, "A boy at my school is gay, and I think he found a boyfriend because he hangs around this other kid a lot and they seem to be happy." Try to leave your opinion about the situation out and create a gap for them to place a reaction. What you're listening for is anger, fear, happiness, or disinterest. Here are some examples of each:

Anger: "You have a gay kid at your school? Who? I'll call the principle right now. There is no place for that kind of thing in school!" or "God will punish that boy. I feel sorry for his parents!"

Fear: "Oh, I hope he doesn't have HIV," or "Are you friends with him? Be careful."

Happiness: "Oh, good! I hope that you and your friends don't make fun of him."

Disinterest: "That's nice, honey. Did you remember to do your homework last night?"

Of those examples, the only one that would throw a red flag for me would be the angry one. The fear response might be a clue that this person will also have that fear with you and that you'll need to make sure to be prepared with some facts around HIV or some assurances that you're safe from that and from bullying when you do come out.

If they respond with "And how do you feel about that?" drop a sign that you're either disinterested or mildly supportive, then see where that leads.

This testing of the waters will prepare you to make the timing decision about coming out. This is worth repeating: if you're dealing with an angry person and you rely on that person for food and shelter, I strongly advise that you stay closeted until the situation improves or you have the ability to support yourself should things go very badly. Again, remember that until you're legally of age, your parents have a lot of say about what happens to you. Legal and mental health systems are often not set up to protect you from a lot of this fallout, so proceed with caution. That doesn't mean you shouldn't reach out for support or that you're all alone. There are a lot of ways for you to get support safely and, if necessary, anonymously *without* coming out.

Should you decide to proceed, the next steps are to find the right moment to break the news and then do it. Here are some general tips:

- Pick a time when the person you're telling is in a good mood and is free of stress in other parts of their life. If they don't already suspect that you're gay, this could be a large shock to them, so be sensitive to other things going on in their life too. If there never seems to be a good moment, you may just have to take a deep breath and go.
- Let them know that you have something important to talk to them about and you'd like to do it without distractions, so turn off the TV and ask them to put down their cell phones.
- Try to tell people one-on-one unless you know that speaking to several at once (Mom and Dad together, for example) would be smoother. One-on-one is preferred because it allows the person being told to have a reaction that isn't influenced by an audience. It's easier to handle one person's reactions at a time. Use your judgment about this.
- Try not to create a situation where the person you tell now has a secret they cannot keep. For example, it's very difficult for one parent not to tell the other. Your mom and dad are (hopefully) in a trusting, loving relationship. They didn't get that way by keeping secrets from each other, so it may be unrealistic to expect that one will be able to keep the secret from the other forever. They may need each other for support. Tell them one at a time if you prefer, but make sure you don't wait too long between people who would likely support each other. If one of your parents knows the other won't do well with the news, trust them about that. They probably know their spouse as a person better than you know them as a parent. But do ask them for help with getting past this. It is your parent's responsibility to use their adult relationship with their spouse to help them to be ok with this news.
- Be honest, but also be confident. If you know you're gay

but, in the heat of the moment, start waffling about it, perhaps about it being a phase or telling them you're bisexual when you know you're not, you're only making your job harder. They may cling to that as a false hope.

- Be prepared for a lot of emotion. Remember that emotion will cloud reasoning. This is not the time for you to play Sarah Scientist or Larry Lawyer. You are not going to be using this time to reason past emotion. If they ask a lot of angry or fearful questions or make those kinds of statements, *try not to react*. Remain calm and tell them you want to talk to them about it when everyone is calm and has had time to process the news. Set up a time to continue the discussion later. If they seem reasonable, by all means have a conversation with them and speak from your heart. Tell them how long you've known and how difficult it's been to keep the secret from them because you want them to love you for who you really are. Assure them that you are still the same child you've always been. Nothing is changing about you. The only thing that is changing is your honesty about who you really are and who you fall in love with.
- Above all, be patient and compassionate. You've had months (or years) to come to terms with everything. They've only had minutes. Don't react in a way that closes the door for future discussion—even if *they* do! After they've calmed down, you may recommend a resource like this book and/or a local PFLAG chapter in the area for support.
- Have a fallback plan. In case things go very badly, make sure you have a place to stay: with a friend, a relative nearby, a sibling who moved out ahead of you. Get out of the situation and give everyone space to cool down. If you can't make that kind of plan, this might not be the best time to come out.

A Journey, Not an Event

You will probably never be "done" coming out. Each time you start a new job, each time you meet a new friend, each time you check into a hotel with your partner and ask for a single king bed, each time you go to a company party for the first time with your partner, each time you go to the hospital and have to put down an emergency contact and fill out the "relation" question, you will be coming out again.

It doesn't end, but it does get easier. With more and more practice, you'll learn how to handle awkward moments when they happen and to appreciate the increasing number of moments that aren't awkward at all. You'll feel stronger and stronger about being who you are and care less and less about the people who choose to walk away because you'll realize that it's a bigger statement about who *they* are than who *you* are.

You'll mourn the loss of loved ones who decided that loving the real you was too uncomfortable for them, but you'll celebrate the amazing feeling of being loved by new people in your life exactly because of who you really are. Having nothing to hide will liberate you to focus on the things that matter most: finding love, finding fulfilling work, learning and honing a craft, and all the other things you've been forced to put in second place behind keeping a secret. It really was one of the most liberating experiences in my life even though there were bumps along the way. My hope is that this book can smooth some of the bumps for you and for those who love you.

Chapter 13: A Life Worth Living

"Things will get easier, people's minds will change, and you should be alive to see it."

— *Ellen DeGeneres*

Parents of Gay Children

When your child was born and as he or she was growing up, you probably had many moments where you imagined what they would become. Perhaps you saw their interest in nature and imagined a future biologist. Or their interest in legal dramas and imagined a future attorney. Or the way they drew beautiful pictures and wondered if they'd become an accomplished artist. The fact that you now know your child is gay changes *nothing* about the person they will become. Zero. Stop to consider how small a part your heterosexuality plays in the big scheme of who you are as a person, what you do for a living, the friends you have, the impact you have on the world. Your child's homosexuality is the same. It is as big or as small of a deal as you make of it.

I opened this book with a question: Do you think everyone has a right to be happy? As we conclude, I want you to consider that question in light of what you may have learned from reading. When we tell our children that who they love and are attracted to is "wrong," what we're essentially saying is, "If you can't love the gender I'm comfortable with loving, you can't love anyone at all in my presence. So, if I'm to be in your life moving forward, you must live your life without love and, therefore, without happiness." Is this what you want for your child and for your relationship? Search your heart, not your mind.

Own your own discomfort rather than blaming your child for it. He or she will not be able to change who they love, but you can change how you feel about who they love. Do that now before it's too late, before your relationship deteriorates or your child decides that your rejection is the final straw. As one of the most influential people in your child's life, you set the tone for whether this journey will be difficult or easy. If you own any discomfort you're feeling and continue getting support until it's gone, you will get through this and, one day, you'll both be thankful you did.

Gay Readers

In the book *Man's Search for Meaning*, Viktor Frankl writes:

> "[M]ental health is based on a certain degree of tension, the tension between what one has already achieved and what one still ought to accomplish, or the gap between what one is and what one should become. Such a tension is inherent in the human being and therefore is indispensable to mental well-being."[53]

This is a man who should know. He survived the infamous Nazi concentration camp called Auschwitz. He watched many men, women, and children die. Many just succumbed to hard labor, disease, and hopelessness. He credits his survival with a strong awareness of what he had yet to accomplish. In his case, a manuscript he had written was confiscated when he was placed in the camp. He knew he'd need to rewrite it when he regained his freedom, and he occupied his mind by reconstructing bits of it on scraps of paper while he was a prisoner. I can't think of many personal hells as terrible as a Nazi concentration camp. Frankl asserts that the difference between those who lived and many of those who died was that those who felt strongly that they had much left to accomplish in their lives persevered through the illness and depression of the circumstances where others did not.

Nietzsche said, "He who has a *why* to live for can bear almost any *how*." I named this chapter "A Life Worth Living" because it's the message that sums up the book you are about to finish. Your life is worth living. There is an entire planet to explore and thousands of people to meet. There are lives for you to impact and for you to be impacted by. There are inventions or works of art for you to create. There are cures to illnesses for you to find. There are people who need to be led, taught, and held. There is love for you to discover and to share. There are people who need your help. There is a *why* to your life, even if others are telling you differently and you don't know what it is right now. It will be evident soon enough. YOU MATTER.

---

[53] Viktor E. Frankl, *Man's Search for Meaning* (Boston: Beacon Press, 2006): 104.

If you were to cut your life short, there are not only people today who would have holes in their hearts for the rest of their lives, the gifts you've yet to bring to the world will go unrealized. The book you're holding in your hand would not be possible if I'd not made the decision over and over to continue living. My life has challenges *and* it has become very rewarding and fulfilling; I believe I've saved lives—and I'm just getting started. I certainly didn't expect to have that impact when I was in my teens. In fact, earlier I mentioned that this book was the result of a promise I made to Neale Donald Walsch, the author of *Conversations with God*. I think it's the right time for me to tell you that story.

I was in a retreat with him some time ago, and we were having a group discussion. I can't recall the exercise we were doing. I told him and the group that I felt compelled to write a book to help people feel OK with being gay, but I didn't know where to begin and it seemed hopeless. I was intimidated. Here I was telling a very successful author who's sold millions of copies of books that have been translated into many languages that I wanted to be an author. And a man who claimed to have multiple conversations with God on top of it! I halfway expected a smirk and a pat on the head and a "Sure, kid. Good luck."

I'll never forget his response. He got red-faced and yelled, "Don't you FUCKING DARE deprive the world of your wisdom and your story! There are lives to be saved. Write that book. The obstacles will get out of your way when they see you coming." Just like that, it became a mission. It also became clear to me that my giving up was letting the world—and myself—down. What I'd yet to accomplish became my "why" and pulled me through some trying times.

If you believe in God, then think of you finding your "why" as discovering (then ultimately delivering to others) the gifts He gave you. Discovering those gifts may require hardship. Perhaps it won't be a Nazi concentration camp but some other version of hardship. Frankl offers this about the meaning of life:

> "[T]he meaning of life differs from man to man, from day to day and from hour to hour. What matters, therefore, is not the meaning of

life in general but rather the specific meaning of a person's life at a given moment. [...] One should not search for an abstract meaning of life. Everyone has his own specific vocation or mission in life to carry out a concrete assignment which demands fulfillment. Therein he cannot be replaced, nor can his life be repeated. Thus, everyone's task is as unique as is his specific opportunity to implement it.

"As each situation in life represents a challenge to man and presents a problem for him to solve, the question of the meaning of life may actually be reversed. Ultimately, man should not ask what the meaning of his life is, but rather he must recognize that it is *he* who is asked. In a word, each man is questioned by life; and he can only answer to life by *answering for* his own life; to life he can only respond by being responsible."[54]

One day, you will stand with pride on a messy pile of rubble that is your dark past. You will wear your wounds as proud reminders of the obstacles you've overcome, and your pile of rubble will raise you to an elevation where your life's meaning is clear. Now it's my turn to tell you: Don't you FUCKING DARE deprive us of your gifts!

A Final Word

When events happen in our lives, it behooves us to ask ourselves, "Who am I in relation to that?" We always have a choice, no matter how "bad" the event is. Who are we in relation to the experience called "losing a job"? Who do we choose to be in relation to the experience called "having a gay son" or "being a gay son"? We are not always in choice about our events, but we are *always* in choice about who we are in relation to them. Always. So, I'd like to leave you with that thought. I invite you to take control of your participation in this life. You are not a victim of circumstance unless you choose to be. Instead, you are actively deciding whether these events will push you forward or hold you back. Every time. No exceptions.

Lost as I may be in the fog of my own noise and triviality
Grant me clarity
I am standing on the edge of forever.

---

[54] Viktor E. Frankl, *Man's Search for Meaning* (Boston: Beacon Press, 2006): 108.

Blessed be this reawakening
That ends my deadly slumber
To stand fearless on the edge of forever.
Witnessing majesty
Calm in humility
Hope as far as I can see
I Stand on the edge of forever

— Based upon the song Grand Canyon by Puscifer (credit to Maynard James Keenan)

Appendix A: Feeling Words

Sometimes we oversimplify our feelings because we lack the vocabulary, or the words aren't coming to us at the right moment. A key part of empathy is being able to identify our own feelings. How can we possibly imagine the nuanced feelings of another if we cannot identify them in ourselves? The list[55] on the next two pages is intended to jog your brain to consider words to describe your feelings more accurately. If the words seem to be the same to you, I encourage you to explore their definitions.

Please consider that, in your life, the difference between "bitter" and "hateful" may seem subtle, while in someone else's life they are miles apart. As an example, I used to think "jealous" and "envious" meant the same thing. These words are not synonymous with each other. Like the feeling words below, the differences could make a big impact when you learn to apply empathy.

This isn't just a semantics exercise. When you understand your feelings accurately, it helps the conversations *about* those feelings. Have you ever had the experience of having a difficult conversation, but each of you were talking past the other? ("That's not what I said," "Why are you getting so angry?" "I think you're overreacting," etc.) It's likely caused by one or both of you not being clear about your feelings. For example, disappointment can sometimes look like anger. In that situation, it helps to tell the other person, "I'm not angry with you, I'm disappointed." From that place, you can deal with why your expectations weren't met (the real issue) vs. someone feeling like they need to defend themselves from your anger (the misunderstood issue).

A list like the one below can be a real game changer in communication. Hopefully you find it as useful as I do.

---

[55] Richard Niolon, "Feeling Words," PsychPage.com, accessed December 30, 2018, http://www.psychpage.com/learning/library/assess/feelings.html.

Pleasant Feelings

OPEN	HAPPY	ALIVE	GOOD
Understanding	Great	Playful	Calm
Confident	Joyous	Courageous	Peaceful
Reliable	Lucky	Energetic	At ease
Easy	Fortunate	Liberated	Comfortable
Amazed	Delighted	Optimistic	Pleased
Free	Overjoyed	Provocative	Encouraged
Sympathetic	Gleeful	Impulsive	Clever
Interested	Thankful	Free	Surprised
Satisfied	Important	Frisky	Content
Receptive	Festive	Animated	Quiet
Accepting	Ecstatic	Spirited	Certain
Kind	Satisfied	Thrilled	Relaxed
	Glad	Wonderful	Serene
	Cheerful		Free and easy
	Sunny		Bright
	Merry		Blessed
	Elated		Reassured

LOVE	INTERESTED	POSITIVE	STRONG
Loving	Concerned	Eager	Impulsive
Considerate	Affected	Keen	Free
Affectionate	Fascinated	Earnest	Sure
Sensitive	Intrigued	Intent	Certain
Tender	Absorbed	Anxious	Rebellious
Devoted	Inquisitive	Inspired	Unique
Attracted	Nosy	Determined	Dynamic
Passionate	Snoopy	Excited	Tenacious
Admiration	Engrossed	Enthusiastic	Hardy
Warm	Curious	Bold	Secure
Touched		Brave	
Sympathy		Daring	
Close		Challenged	
Loved		Optimistic	
Comforted		Hopeful	
Drawn toward		Confident	

Difficult/Unpleasant Feelings

ANGRY	DEPRESSED	CONFUSED	HELPLESS
Irritated	Lousy	Upset	Incapable
Enraged	Disappointed	Doubtful	Alone
Hostile	Discouraged	Uncertain	Paralyzed
Insulting	Ashamed	Indecisive	Fatigued
Sore	Powerless	Perplexed	Useless
Annoyed	Diminished	Embarrassed	Inferior
Upset	Guilty	Hesitant	Vulnerable
Hateful	Dissatisfied	Shy	Empty
Unpleasant	Miserable	Stupefied	Forced
Offensive	Detestable	Disillusioned	Hesitant
Bitter	Repugnant	Unbelieving	Despair
Aggressive	Despicable	Skeptical	Frustrated
Resentful	Disgusting	Distrustful	Distressed
Inflamed	Abominable	Misgiving	Woeful
Provoked	Terrible	Lost	Pathetic
Incensed	In despair	Unsure	Tragic
Infuriated	Sulky	Uneasy	In a stew
Cross	Bad	Pessimistic	Dominated
Worked up	A sense of loss	Tense	
Boiling			
Fuming			
Indignant			

INDIFFERENT	AFRAID	HURT	SAD
Insensitive	Fearful	Crushed	Tearful
Dull	Terrified	Tormented	Sorrowful
Nonchalant	Suspicious	Deprived	Pained
Neutral	Anxious	Pained	Grief
Reserved	Alarmed	Tortured	Anguish
Weary	Panic	Dejected	Desolate
Bored	Nervous	Rejected	Desperate
Preoccupied	Scared	Injured	Pessimistic
Cold	Worried	Offended	Unhappy
Disinterested	Frightened	Afflicted	Lonely
Lifeless	Timid	Aching	Grieved
	Shaky	Victimized	Mournful
	Restless	Heartbroken	Dismayed
	Doubtful	Agonized	
	Threatened	Appalled	
	Cowardly	Humiliated	
	Quaking	Wronged	
	Menaced	Alienated	
	Wary		

Appendix B: Recommended Resources

Because the Internet stands still for no one, links expire and grow stale. I will list links to main organizations below, but links that are intended to direct you to a specific article, video, or other resource will be linked on my website, **oktobegaybook.com**. I will strive to keep the site up-to-date with current articles, quotes, links to videos, and other resources.

Dealing with Change

- *When Everything Changes, Change Everything,* by Neale Donald Walsch
- *The Power of TED,* by David Emerald
- *The Anatomy of Peace,* by The Arbinger Institute
- *Transitions: Making Sense of Life's Changes,* by William Bridges
- *Emotional Freedom: Liberate Yourself from Negative Emotions and Transform Your Life,* by Judith Orloff, M.D.

Reddit: www.reddit.com + rest of URL below

I find that the people in many of these subreddits are awesome and supportive, and the standard warnings and disclaimers still apply. You may see sexual content and profanity. Their standard policy is that Reddit is not intended for those under thirteen. Reddit is a giant community full of all kinds of people. Not everyone on Reddit is awesome, but moderated subreddits are usually pretty good about keeping things sane. When I weighed the pros vs. the cons of including these links, there was no doubt the good of connection outweighs the risk of offending anyone.

- /r/lgbteens
- /r/comingout
- /r/ainbow
- /r/actuallesbians
- /r/asexuality
- /r/bisexual
- /r/gay

- /r/gaymers
- /r/genderqueer

Bullying/Cyberbullying

- Facebook Bullying Prevention Hub: www.facebook.com/safety/bullying
- www.stopBullying.gov
- www.cyberbullying.org
- www.ryanpatrickhalligan.org; *Ryan's Story,* by John P. Halligan
- www.pacer.org/bullying

Religion

- **Christianity**
  - *Gay and Okay: A Conservative Christian's Mind Change,* by John W Brown
  - *Space at the Table: Conversations Between an Evangelical Theologian and His Gay Son,* by Brad and Drew Harper
  - *The Children Are Free: Reexamining the Biblical Evidence on Same-Sex Relationships,* by Reverend Jeff Miner and John Tyler Connoley
  - *Conversations With God,* by Neale Donald Walsch
  - *Kidnapped for Christ* (Documentary; see www.kidnappedforchrist.com)
  - *For the Bible Tells Me So* (Documentary; see www.forthebibletellsmeso.org)
  - *The Church and the Homosexual,* by John J. McNeill

- **Hinduism**
  - Queering India: Same-Sex Love and Eroticism in Indian Culture and Society, edited by Ruth Vanita

- **Islam**
  - www.mpvusa.org/lgbtqi-resources
  - www.mpvusa.org/sexuality-diversity

- o Homosexuality in Islam: Critical Reflections on Gay, Lesbian, and Transgender Muslims, by Scott Siraj al-Haqq Kugle

- **Mormonism**
  - o Latter Days: (fictional movie)
  - o affirmation.org (clicking the "Find Affinity Groups" link at the bottom will take you to many additional resources.

- **General Religion**
  - o *Behold, I Make All Things New: What Do the Sacred Texts of Judaism, Christianity, and Islam Really Say in Regard to Human Sexuality,* edited by The Reverend Loraine Tulleken B.Th (Hons) and The Reverend JP Mokgethi-Heath B.Th (Hons)
  - o *Boy Erased* (Conversion therapy movie based on a true story)
  - o *Trevor* (Movie)

General LGBT Topics (Politics, History, and Miscellaneous)

- *The Right Side of History: 100 Years of LGBTQ Activism,* by Adrian Brooks
- *Virtually Normal,* by Andrew Sullivan
- *A Place at the Table: The Gay Individual in American Society,* by Bruce Bawer
- *Is It a Choice? Answers to the Most Frequently Asked Questions About Gay and Lesbian People,* by Eric Marcus
- *Positively Gay: New Approaches to Gay and Lesbian Life,* edited by Betty Berzon, Ph.D.

Suicide Prevention

- The Trevor Project: (Check website for the most up-to-date hours and the availability of various contact methods.)

- o www.theTrevorProject.com
- o 1-866-488-7386 (24/7/365)
- o Text START to 678678 (7 days per week between noon – 1 a.m. ET and 9 a.m. – 10 p.m. PT)
- o Online chat is available on the site during same hours as texting above.
- *Reddit:* www.reddit.com [use rest of URL below]
  - o /r/suicidewatch
  - o /r/itgetsbetter
  - o /r/lgbthavens/
  - o /r/troubledteens

Support Groups and Collections of Resources

- Brandon Shire: www.brandonshire.com/lgbt-youth-organizations/
- Gay Straight Alliances: gsanetwork.org
- Parents and Friends of Lesbians and Gays (PFLAG)
  - o Search for a local chapter on www.pflag.org
- Muslims: www.mpvusa.org/lgbtqi-resources/

Transgender/Gender Identity

- GLAAD: www.glaad.org/transgender/resources
- For Parents: www.mothersoftransgenderchildren.wordpress.com

Straight but Attracted to Same-Gender Sex

- *Is My Husband Gay, Straight, or Bi?: A Guide for Women Concerned about Their Men,* by Joe Kort
- www.straightguise.com